FROM WELLBEING TO WELLDOING

FROM WELLBEING TO WELLDOING

HOW TO THINK, LEARN AND BE WELL

ABBY
OSBORNE

LOTI
VENABLES

KAREN
ANGUS-COLE

1 Oliver's Yard
55 City Road
London EC1Y 1SP

2455 Teller Road
Thousand Oaks
California 91320

Unit No 323-333, Third Floor, F-Block
International Trade Tower
Nehru Place, New Delhi – 110 019

8 Marina View Suite 43-053
Asia Square Tower 1
Singapore 018960

Editor: Kate Keers
Assistant editor: Sahar Jamfar
Production editor: Nicola Marshall
Copyeditor: Tom Bedford
Proofreader: Sharon Cawood
Indexer: C&M Digitals (P) Ltd, Chennai, India
Marketing manager: Maria Omena
Cover design: Sheila Tong
Typeset by: C&M Digitals (P) Ltd, Chennai, India
Printed in the UK

Library of Congress Control Number: 2023932925

British Library Cataloguing in Publication data

A catalogue record for this book is available from the British Library

ISBN 978-1-5297-6893-0
ISBN 978-1-5297-6892-3 (pbk)

At Sage we take sustainability seriously. Most of our products are printed in the UK using responsibly sourced papers and boards. When we print overseas we ensure sustainable papers are used as measured by the Paper Chain Project grading system. We undertake an annual audit to monitor our sustainability.

For Sam, Rosa, Grace, Louie and Ike.
Keep growing, learning and embracing all that life presents you with.

Contents

Prologue

Learners often think that their teachers are their greatest resource; whilst writing this book, we have frequently been reminded that, as teachers, our learners are *our* greatest resource. Many of the tried-and-tested Welldoing strategies included in this book are the result of working with a diverse range of students over a number of years. These students have developed strategies, or adapted those that we have shared with them, in response to things that *they* have found challenging. We have been truly humbled by the scope and sheer creativity of the Welldoing strategies our students have generated. This breadth of shared experience has really enabled us to consolidate Welldoing and subsequently promote a much more flexible, holistic and sustainable approach to overcoming barriers we all face.

Whilst Welldoing can help us all to better manage the pressures of learning, we must highlight that this is not a therapeutic book. Although we are teachers, we are not, for example, qualified medical professionals, psychologists or psychotherapists. This book is intended to help you to identify and use strategies to manage your multi-faceted life *before* life becomes too much and you become unwell. Therefore, if you are at the point where you need professional help, medical attention or have been referred to any medical services in order to manage your wellbeing, it is important to use these services and access specialised professional support. You may find that the advice you receive from health professionals, when you work with them, can be used in conjunction with the strategies in this book.

We have used many of the Welldoing strategies outlined in this book to support our own learning and working; using them has helped us to produce the book itself! There have been many occasions where we have hit a brick wall, felt unable to move forward, doubted ourselves and struggled to stay motivated. We have also all struggled to juggle writing with our busy, multi-faceted lives. We are sure many of you can relate to these feelings when facing your own challenges. Time and time again, we had to remind ourselves to return to the very focus of the book and to try different ways of working. We had to remind ourselves not to be afraid to step away and to employ a different or more flexible approach when the way in which we were working had actually stopped working.

Through our shared experience of working together, we have not only been able to broaden our toolkits and share our strategies, but we have learnt the importance of frequently reminding one another to think flexibly and holistically in order to effectively problem-solve the hurdles that we face. The most important thing that has been reinforced for us in creating this book is that, actually, there is no ideal or specific way of approaching or completing tasks – and also that the initial approaches we adopt often need to flex and change as we progress. We are very grateful for the many colleagues and students who have encouraged us to practise what we preach by thinking outside the box, challenging what we already know and take for granted, and rethinking our ability to overcome some of the common challenges that we all face on a daily basis. Therefore, we encourage you to free yourself up to also think in this more flexible, holistic way and to adopt this Welldoing approach for yourself.

Who is this book for?

This book is primarily aimed at **students**, whether you are studying at university, college or school. The **Welldoing approach** works for **all** students and subject disciplines and is applicable throughout your journey as a learner from GCSE to post-graduate study. Welldoing supports our wellbeing through the very things that we do, whether that be learning, working or even managing our day-to-day lives. It helps us to remain conscious of maintaining our wellbeing, even during stressful and busy periods in our life, by actively considering *how* we approach tasks. The Welldoing strategies within this book will support you to actively overcome a range of challenges that you might be facing with your learning and wellbeing, be it the way you tackle an assignment, juggle pending deadlines or consider healthy sleep solutions. But they can also simply be used to help you to study smarter. Whilst the Welldoing strategies primarily focus on learning in this book, many can be applied to other areas of life beyond the classroom. Therefore, the Welldoing approach provides more than a manual for study; it introduces a range of transferable strategies to help to ensure that you thrive at home and at work as well as at school, college or university: to think, learn and be well.

This book is also useful for a range of people whose role it is to **support students** with their learning, primarily **teachers** and **parents**.

Busy teachers who are interested in promoting more **inclusive approaches to learning** in their classrooms, but perhaps don't know where to start, can benefit from bringing the Welldoing approach into their classrooms. The Welldoing strategies in this book can be introduced to students gradually, modelled by the teacher, and scaffolded in order to help students develop independence, greater resilience and self-regulation. The Welldoing approach recognises that students play a vital role in developing inclusive classrooms and steers students towards healthy habits for learning, studying and relaxing. Finally, teachers may also find the book a useful tool to manage their own hefty workload and juggle work–life balance in a Welldoing way.

We feel there are very few learning and study-related books that directly help parents to support their children's learning. As busy mums, we ourselves have all been faced with the overwhelming feeling of wanting to **help and support our family's education**, but have not always had the time or know-how to do this. Therefore, we hope that the Welldoing strategies in this book provide an accessible, helpful and solution-focused approach that parents can draw on to support their children to thrive and become the best versions of themselves in the Welldoing way.

Who we are

Abby has extensive experience in mentoring and tutoring students in secondary, further and higher education. She currently works as the Assessment and Feedback Development Lead at the University of Bath's Centre for Learning and Teaching, supporting the development of teaching, learning and assessment. She has a background in inclusive education and experience in supporting student wellbeing both within and beyond the curriculum. Abby also works as an educational consultant, most recently working with Cambridge Assessment International Education, developing educational guidance for international teachers.

Karen has a number of years' experience teaching in UK secondary schools and tutoring students. She is currently a Lecturer in Education at the University of Bath and Director of Studies for the Education with Psychology degree. She also works as an education consultant designing learning materials for students, as well as professional development workshops for teaching staff. She has created BBC Bitesize revision resources for secondary school students, conducted research projects with the University of Cambridge, as well as worked as a teacher trainer and resource developer for Cambridge Assessment International Education and Cambridge University Press.

Loti is a Special Educational Needs (SEN) specialist teacher within a mainstream secondary school, delivering Alternative Provision to a range of vulnerable, disadvantaged and SEN students. With a degree in Illustration and Graphics, she applies her visual way of seeing the world to produce supporting academic materials and pastoral guides within her department. Loti has worked for over two decades in teaching, working as an art specialist within a SEN setting, as a secondary school SEN coordinator and as an art teacher delivering GCSE and A level teaching. Recently she has combined both skill sets to deliver Art as an Alternative Provision, with a focus on mentoring, social and life skills.

Acknowledgements

First and foremost, we would like to thank all of the students we have worked with over the years. Without your foresight, creativity and resilience, this book would not have been possible.

We would also like to thank our friends and colleagues, Paul Ellis, Jo Hatt, Liz Beavan and Frances Wood. Without your encouragement and support, we would not have been able to finish this book. Thanks to Kate, Sahar and Nicola at Sage for your patience and invaluable guidance.

Thanks finally to our families and friends for the motivational reminders and for accepting that we may not have always had the time and capacity to be there fully for you when immersed in the writing of this book. We also have to acknowledge the four-legged members of our families for keeping us grounded and reminding us of what is truly important.

Welcome to Welldoing

From wellbeing to Welldoing: What is Welldoing and how is it different from wellbeing?

Wellbeing is something we are all becoming increasingly aware of, whether this is in the form of taking time out for ourselves, being more mindful or putting in place good habits to reduce our stress levels. Yet, in spite of this increasing recognition, wellbeing is still frequently regarded as something that sits *outside* of or beyond learning, as an antidote to the pressures and strains of study that we all experience.

Whilst wellbeing practices such as mindfulness, exercise and healthy nutrition are important steps in ensuring good mental health, we believe that we can do even more to support our wellbeing by adapting the very ways in which we learn, think and study.

Welldoing exists at the intersection between wellbeing and learning (**Figure 1.1**). We can manage our wellbeing through the very ways in which we learn and vice versa. Welldoing is essentially about tailoring, adapting and refining the way in which we approach or '*do*' tasks, allowing this to shift and fluctuate depending on our context, what we need to achieve or how we might be feeling.

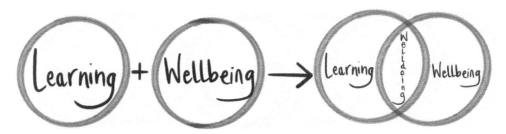

Figure 1.1   What is Welldoing?

CAPTION: Welldoing exists at the intersection between wellbeing and learning.

Why is the Welldoing approach important and how will it help you?

1. **Welldoing promotes effective learning which is tailored to work for you and adapted to your changing needs.**

   As a society we often have ideal ways of conceptualising how we should best learn. As an example, we may default to assuming that the best place to learn is at a desk with bright lighting, a clear space and silence, but this working setup might not always suit our needs or requirements. By embracing Welldoing and therefore by being more flexible in our approach and opening ourselves up to different methods and modes of working, we can begin to take greater control of our learning, identifying what works for us. Building on this, we can evolve our own personalised, highly adaptive toolkit, which can be applied to multiple working and learning contexts. Just as an artist mixes colours to find the right shade or hue, Welldoing embraces a creative approach to make learning work for each of us.

2. Welldoing can help you to overcome commonly experienced barriers to learning.

There are numerous barriers that students face with their learning, and although these barriers vary from student to student there are many things that we have found are quite common. Welldoing can give you the toolkit to overcome these barriers independently and therefore take greater control of your learning. For example, perhaps there were things you were afraid to ask or were never explicitly told at school (how to plan your work, how to write a paragraph), or things you were told were important ('be organised' or 'manage your time') but were never told *how* to do this. Welldoing provides you with options, offering multiple means of overcoming challenges, rather than a one-size-fits-all approach. Look at the Contents to see the range of areas this Welldoing book covers, from managing stress, to planning and writing, to efficient revision approaches and how to work efficiently and effectively in groups, plus many others.

3. Welldoing offers a transferable approach beyond the classroom to help us to manage everyday thinking, working and living.

The Welldoing approach can be used to help us reflect on *how* we approach tasks in multiple areas of our lives. It can also help us to actively draw on strategies used in one area of our lives to help us manage other areas which we might be finding challenging. For example, if you feel that you could be better at organising your studies, Welldoing encourages you to reflect on areas of your life where you have put in place or developed effective strategies to support organisation: If you're someone who finds it easier to tidy and clean your room or home by breaking this down into manageable steps, you may find this approach is also applicable to your studies and that breaking down assignment- or revision-related tasks in the same way enables you to make it manageable, boost your motivation and enable you to see progress.

Therefore, most of the strategies outlined in this book are applicable to a range of contexts beyond that of the world of study. Look at the **Welldoing4home** and **Welldoing4work** explanations in **The Welldoing toolkit** section starting on page 7, and whilst using the book keep an eye out for the **Welldoing4home** and **Welldoing4work** icons.

Key features to help you navigate the book's chapters

Here we briefly outline the key features that you will see in every chapter.

Is this chapter for me?

Each chapter begins with a few questions you can ask yourself to see if the chapter covers Welldoing strategies which are likely to be useful to you. Remember that even if a chapter does not seem relevant to you at the moment, this may change over time. Learning (and life) can present different hurdles as our circumstances change. It is also worth noting that even if a chapter does not seem immediately useful to you, it may still contain some potentially useful strategies, as explained in **How to use this book: Make this book your own!** below.

The big picture

The big picture sets the scene for each chapter and will give you an overview of what the focus of the chapter will be. We outline the key challenges students often face linked to the chapter's focus, before setting out how we will draw on the Welldoing approach to help you problem-solve and find creative solutions to effectively overcome these challenges.

Check in on your Welldoing...

We have included a number of opportunities to Check in on your Welldoing throughout the book. These features provide you with the chance to take stock and really reflect on the overall Welldoing focus of the chapter or section in relation to your own needs and situation.

Pause for thought

Peppered throughout the chapters, the Pause for thought feature offers you a chance to stop and think about how specific Welldoing strategies that have just been shared could apply to your own context.

Student voices

‘ Throughout the book, you will find quotes from real-life students who we have had the pleasure of working with (and learning from). This has allowed us to capture and share with you students' lived experiences of applying the Welldoing approach and strategies as a way to overcome their own working and learning challenges. ’

Bear in mind

The Bear in mind feature provides a useful reminder that sometimes a new approach or way of working, although useful, might also come with a small caveat; some strategies might, in certain circumstances, impact on the way we do things or come with certain stipulations. When we change the way we do something in any area of our lives, this change needs to be thought about so that we get the most out of it. Whilst the Welldoing strategies encourage small tweaks to the way we approach things, we want you to think about what is working for you to make sure that the Welldoing approach helps you to embrace Welldoing in *your* own way.

Key take aways

This feature summarises the chapter in a few bullet points, highlighting the chapter's key messages and take aways. Use this feature as a quick reminder or recap of what the chapter has covered, or when you need a quick refresher if you are returning to a chapter you have read previously.

The authors' approach to Welldoing

This feature gives you an insight into how we, the authors, use the Welldoing strategies in our own work and home lives, demonstrating the universal nature of Welldoing as a tool which can help us all to thrive. It will also give you a sense of how we constantly make adaptions to the way we work; indeed, we don't think that we would have been able to write this book without drawing on the approach ourselves.

My blank canvas

Each My blank canvas feature includes a blank space on the page
to encourage you to **Pick and mix** and **Develop your combo** (see
Welldoing toolkit) of particular Welldoing strategies and ideas
which may be of use to you and that you would like to try, explore and potentially revisit – even
from other chapters. Just as an artist mixes colours on a paint pallet to get just the right shade
or hue of a colour, we encourage you to be creative, bold and explore what works for you.

We also encourage you to use the **My blank canvas** spaces to revisit, review and
refine those strategies which might be most useful to you. Even when we find a new strategy, we often default back to what we know because we are creatures of habit, even when
this may no longer be helpful to us (Hora and Oleson, 2017; Sauvé et al., 2016). Ironically,
we sometimes overlook or forget strategies when we need them most. Therefore, use the
My blank canvas spaces to help remind you to revisit and refine your approaches to
Welldoing.

Do also add your own strategies; whilst we have tried to provide a number of different
approaches to tackling common challenges, we recognise that the number of Welldoing strategies is in no way limited to what we have managed to capture within this book. We are constantly adding to our own repertoire, through personal reflection as well as through working
with students, and we are never more excited than when we find a new and creative way of
overcoming a challenge.

We have also added a template in **Chapter 10** for you to pull together all your
favourite Welldoing strategies from across the book into one space. See our tempting
Template 22: Welldoing your way!

If you have your own tried-and-tested Welldoing strategies that you would like to share
with us, please use the hashtag #Welldoing. Welldoing as an approach works best when
we work together, share ideas and support one another to be the most effective versions of
ourselves.

Further resources

This feature will signpost you to further resources which may be of interest to
you. Where relevant, we will also signpost you to further services which may be
able to provide additional guidance and support.

The Welldoing toolkit

Before you begin exploring our Welldoing strategies, we would like to introduce you to the Welldoing toolkit. The Welldoing toolkit is designed to work alongside the Welldoing strategies which are outlined throughout the book's chapters; the toolkit will enable you to better tailor and adapt the strategies to suit *your* way of working, as well as giving you greater confidence to also decide and discard what *doesn't* work for you.

Look out for the following Welldoing toolkit icons when exploring the book. Remember that, whilst the strategies themselves within each chapter are important, even more fundamental to the Welldoing approach is learning how to best combine and adapt the strategies to overcome any hurdles we may face.

Pick and mix

A really fundamental but often overlooked aspect of learning is that we need to identify what doesn't work for us as much as what does. This book will introduce you to numerous strategies to tackle various aspects of your learning, working and everyday life, but it is important to remember to *select those strategies that work for you.* We may find that different strategies work at different times or in different contexts; a fundamental aspect of the Welldoing approach is to **Pick and mix** the Welldoing strategies, just as you would with a selection of sweets: use the strategies which you feel most suit your needs and feel free to leave behind those that are not helpful to you.

It is also worth remembering that sometimes we may have a way of working or learning that has become a habit, a go-to approach for us that feels like it works every time or has become our default as we have never really explored any other options. Remember to be open-minded when you **Pick and mix** your strategies as sometimes our needs change and an approach that may have worked for us in the past may stop working – and vice versa.

Develop your combo

Also fundamental to Welldoing is our ability to combine and layer different strategies. Although many of the Welldoing strategies in this book can stand alone, in order for them to be most impactful it is often best to combine them with others. This might include building your combo of strategies outlined within one chapter or section,

or working across chapters to combine them in a way that works for you. The possibilities are endless!

Think about the analogy of when we order a burger; we all have our personal combination or combo of ingredients and toppings that we like to layer up in different amounts or quantities to build our favourite, tasty burger. It is exactly the same when using the Welldoing approach and choosing and combining Welldoing strategies. Remember that your combo may be different depending on your needs or circumstances, and also that this can shift over time. There is no limit to how personalised your combos can be, or even how often they might need to change.

Turn up (or down!) the dial

Turning up (or down) the dial is another tool for supporting us to think, learn and work more flexibly. This aspect of the Welldoing toolkit relates to our ability to alter or adapt the *amount* we may be using a Welldoing strategy. Sometimes we can assume that a strategy does not work for us, but adapting the extent to which we use the strategy is also really important. As an example, if we realise that light is important to us and affects our motivation and focus, we might find that by adapting the actual *level* of light or even changing the light *hue*, we can also increase our motivation and focus. Therefore, don't be afraid to Turn up the dial (or turn it down) when testing out the Welldoing strategies, in order to get a more nuanced understanding of how you work and learn best.

Welldoing4home and Welldoing4work

It can be easy to think that we require a very different set of strategies or skills in different areas of our lives. Therefore, it's not unusual for us to separate out groups of skills into those that we think are study related, those that link to our employment and working lives, and the whole range of strategies which we use to manage our home lives. However, there is much more overlap between these strategies than we might first realise; central to the Welldoing approach is the recognition that if we identify Welldoing strategies which work for study or which work for us whilst we're employed, frequently these strategies can shift and be adapted so that we can apply them in *multiple* contexts. Actively considering the transferability of Welldoing strategies between multiple different contexts also better enables us to cement effective working habits. This is really important because it can be very difficult to cement new behaviours or habits without revisiting them multiple times; we may default back to strategies that we have used previously but that actually aren't particularly efficient, effective or sustainable.

Therefore, when exploring the strategies outlined in this book we would encourage you to try and break down some of the artificial distinctions we naturally make between the skills we believe we need for study, employment or day-to-day life. Instead, think about the strategies as being much more adaptive, flexible and transferable. As an example, you may have **Picked**, **mixed** and developed a **Combo** of strategies, such as using a table for assignment planning combined with some colour coding to group the different points you want to make. As well as providing a useful method for working on an assignment, these Welldoing strategies could equally be effectively used in the workplace when planning a report that you have to produce or when preparing to deliver a presentation or speech. Furthermore, the same strategies could just as effectively be applied in your home life if you're trying to plan a trip abroad or an event you are organising.

Common sensory approach

Throughout this book, we make reference to the importance of our environment and demonstrate how this can subtly shape and impact on our ability to think, learn and work. We all use our senses to make *sense* of the world around us: our sight, hearing, touch, taste and smell directly influence how we perceive and interact with both our environment and other people. In spite of this, we often overlook how significant our senses can be in shaping and boosting our learning potential.

We would encourage you to apply a **Common sensory approach** and reflect on how you can use your senses to better harness your environment to boost motivation, concentration and focus. Whilst you will find numerous strategies throughout the book which draw on our common sensory approach, we have also included it here as part of the Welldoing toolkit; this approach works well when combined with other strategies and is an essential ingredient in building our tailored approach to smart thinking, learning and working.

Don't be afraid to go beyond an often idealised version of what a 'good' learning environment may look like; whilst some us may thrive when we have a clear desk, bright lighting and silence, many of us may benefit from making tweaks to our learning environment which actually challenge the status quo; if you find loud music, getting snug in a blanket or having the television on in the background actually *helps* you to focus, then don't be afraid to embrace this.

Micro and macro levels

Many of the Welldoing strategies can be applied at both a **macro** and **micro** level. For example, you might find the strategy of **Breaking-down tasks** helpful at a macro level when juggling tasks that you need to complete across various parts of your life linked to your study, work and home. At the same time, you can apply the same strategy at a micro level, when breaking down the steps you need to finish off a piece of work or task you are working on.

In other words, what makes the strategy of breaking down most powerful is the transferable nature of the approach and its ability to help us make any area of our lives more manageable. When you find a strategy that is particularly useful, consider whether you can apply this in different contexts, as described in **Welldoing4home** and **Welldoing4work**, as well as whether you can apply it in its broadest sense or in a way that is very focused and specific.

SOS: Save our spoons

Central to the Welldoing approach is our ability to save our energies and harness this efficiently so that we achieve our goals in a way that is sustainable. For multiple reasons, it is quite normal to find that some days we may feel we have more energy than others, but this fluctuating level of energy is hard to conceptualise, keep track of and measure. Which brings us to 'spoons'.

The Spoons Theory was created by Christine Miserandino to describe the challenge of managing day-to-day life with a limited amount of energy associated with chronic illness (Miserandino, 2020). The Spoons Theory has provided an invaluable tool to thousands of individuals who need to think carefully about the energy that they are able to expend, whether this is linked to a chronic health condition, disability or other life circumstances beyond their control. The theory has also gained increasing attention as a useful tool to help us *all* better regulate the energy available to us.

The analogy of **spoons** as finite 'blocks' of energy has really helped to provide us, the authors, with a useful, everyday metaphor for expressing the energy available to us as something more tangible that we can learn to plan for, regulate and control. Communicating how many spoons we've had to one another has been vital for completing this book!

Spoons are therefore central to the Welldoing approach and enable us to expend our energy in a way that is effective, impactful and sustainable, so we want to share the spoons approach with you so that you can also use it as part of *your* Welldoing toolkit.

Thinking in terms of tangible 'spoons' can remind us to try and conserve our energies and develop more sustainable approaches to learning, working and living. Many of the Welldoing strategies explored throughout the book will help you to **save your spoons**, whether this is in the form of employing smart working habits, increasing your awareness of your environment and how it might affect how energised you feel or learning when to take a step back, recharge and recuperate when necessary.

How to use this book: Make this book your own!

This book can be read from start to finish like a traditional book. Or it can be read more fluidly; feel free to dip in and out of the text in any order, read whole chapters in one sitting, or just spend five minutes looking at one or two strategies.

A holistic approach

Whilst this book comprises distinct chapters, each with its own key focus on a common challenge linked to learning and study, it is really important to develop a *holistic* approach to problem-solving the hurdles that we might face. Use the Contents page and chapter headings as a guide to signpost you to specific areas you may want to tackle, but remember that, at its most effective, this book will be most useful to you if you think outside the box and explore strategies that perhaps you might not immediately associate with the specific challenge you face. For example, if you have picked up this book because you'd like to develop some effective strategies for managing the pressures of presenting, your first thought might be to head straight to the chapter that tackles this. To really benefit, however, it is important to recognise that almost every challenge you face is made up of *multiple* smaller hurdles. Thus, *only* looking at the **Walking a tightrope** chapter might not fully support you with addressing this challenge. When you are faced with managing the pressures of presenting, dipping into the chapter related to this challenge *will* be helpful but (although it may not immediately seem like an obvious approach) you may also find it useful to look at some of the Welldoing strategies outlined in **Stress-free learning (well almost!)** or in **Cognitively comfy learning**.

Templates

As well as the **Check in on your Welldoing**, **Pause for thought** and **My blank canvas** features that are included within the main chapters, we have included a Templates chapter at the end of the book. This provides you with example templates aimed at helping you with every aspect of learning, from planning for an assignment to revising for a test. These templates have been tried and tested and used by a diverse range of students. However, we encourage you to adapt them as needed and make them your own to fully embrace the Welldoing approach. Adapting the templates will help you to ensure that they work as effectively as possible to scaffold *your* thinking and learning. And remember, a template to support your thinking for planning for an assignment may also be easily adapted to help you in an employment context or to manage an aspect of your home life.

Revisit, remind, review

Don't forget to keep returning to the book. This is central to the Welldoing approach. In order to cement effective and sustainable ways of thinking, learning, living and working, it is important to keep going back and **revisiting** strategies so that they become habitual. We are only human and with the best will in the world, we often forget to revisit those strategies that have been useful to us in the past.

We also might find that we simply forget to draw on effective strategies when we need them most. There is always so much going on in our lives, we can easily forget the power of **reminding** ourselves of things we have done in the past that have worked – we have just moved on and gradually forgotten about them. We have included a specific template in **Chapter 10** to help you carve out a space where you can make a note of the strategies, so that they are gathered together for when you need them most. See **Template 23** as a reminder to **Take your Welldoing up a level** when you might need it most.

As we say throughout the book, **review** the strategies and work out what works for you at a specific point in your studies, home life or work. Remember to tweak the strategies you use to reflect your ever-changing circumstances.

Therefore, follow our mantra when using the Welldoing approach: **revisit, remind, review** to make Welldoing work for you!

So make this book your own!

We encourage you to move freely through the book, drawing on the **Welldoing toolkit** by **Pick and mixing** and **Developing your combo** across the chapters to develop a Welldoing approach which is just right for you.

Turn up or down the dial when you review and revisit strategies, think about using strategies at **Micro and macro levels**, highlight your favourite strategies,

Develop your combo in creative ways and scribble notes in the spaces that we have provided – or anywhere you like really!

Use the book in a way that is helpful for *you* and which supports you and your own personal Welldoing.

Finding a pathway through the book: Signposted routes for getting started when you feel lost and are not sure where to begin

If you really are not sure where to start, we have mapped out some possible routes through the book based on challenges which students have commonly identified. If you think you want to perfect the art of not being a perfectionist or would like a helping hand with overcoming information overload and analysis paralysis, then our suggested signposted routes below might provide you with a useful starting point for developing a **Combo** that works for you.

These are *suggested* routes and it is likely you will work out your own pathway through the book as you become more confident at adopting, adapting and applying Welldoing strategies to the varied challenges you face.

Perfect the art of not being a perfectionist! Step right this way...

- Time can be our worst enemy when we are prone to perfectionism! Have a look at **The 4 Ds of do, defer, delegate and delete** (**Chapter 4**) to help you prioritise tasks rather than trying to achieve everything. Our strategies, **Under promise and over deliver**, **Deadlines and targets window** and **Email delay** (all in **Chapter 4**) provide a selection of practical approaches to learning to manage the expectations we place on ourselves.
- Taking note of what you have achieved is really important and can sometimes be easy to overlook when we are natural perfectionists. Have a look at our **Making good time: Taking note of your progress** in **Chapter 3** to help you to see everything you have achieved.
- Our **Fear of the blank page** strategies (**Chapter 5**) can help to free you up when starting work, particularly if you feel pressure to produce perfect work as soon as you start writing.
- If your perfectionism leads to over-thinking and over-worrying, you might find it useful to look at our **Worry management** strategies, as well as our **Welldoing approach to active relaxing** in **Chapter 4** to help you to switch off and unwind.
- We also recommend checking the **If something's worth doing, it's (sometimes) worth doing less well!** strategy in **Chapter 4** and combining this with our **Save our spoons** approach to Welldoing throughout the book.

Overcoming analysis paralysis: Step right this way...

- Take a look at **Chapter 2: Cognitively comfy learning**. This will help you to utilise and harness your senses and your environment to maximum effect to reduce your analysis paralysis.
- Our **Fear of the blank page** strategies (**Chapter 5**) will help you to overcome over-thinking the process of getting started.
- You might also like to try our recipe for **Making, planning and writing a piece of CAKE** in **Chapter 6** to help you break down the stages of planning and writing.
- If reading sparks your analysis paralysis, you may also like to try our **Reading shopping baskets and shopping lists** (**Chapter 6**) as well as our **Zoom reading** strategies in **Chapter 5**.
- If your analysis paralysis leads you to over-think and worry, you might find our **Worry management** strategies in **Chapter 4** provide a useful starting point.

Prevent the procrastination: Step right this way...

- Making sure you are **Cognitively comfy** is vital. Take a look at the strategies in **Chapter 2** to help you **Move**, **Manage** and **Micro-manage** your environment so you give yourself the best possible chance of connecting with your work.
- Our **Dabble technique** in **Chapter 3** is a procrastinator's dream! Combine this with the **Breaking it down** and **Quick wins** strategies, also in **Chapter 3**, for maximum effect.
- Take a look at our strategies for **Managing pace** in **Chapter 3** – sometimes adrenaline builds nearer a deadline which makes it easier to kick start your work.

How to *get over* over-thinking and over-worrying: Step right this way...

- Try our **Cognitively comfy learning** strategies in **Chapter 2**. This will help you to harness your environment to better ground you, with the right sensory inputs helping you to spend less time in your head. Combine this with our **Active relaxing** (**Chapter 4**) strategies for maximum impact.
- If you are prone to worry and find this impacts on your everyday life including your studies, then have a look at our **Worry management** strategies in **Chapter 4**.
- Our Safety nets to thriving rather than surviving public speaking and presenting (Chapter 8) and our Hurdle free approach to group work (Chapter 9) will help you to actively manage any worries you are experiencing linked to working with others.

Cognitively comfy learning

Manage your environment to boost your learning potential

Is this chapter for me?

- Does the environment you are working in sometimes make it hard to focus on the task you want to be getting on with?

- Do you often find yourself zoning out, getting distracted or daydreaming when trying to study?

- Are you sensitive to certain sounds, textures, smells and tastes?

Cognitively comfy learning: The big picture

Comfy and learning may not be words that you would immediately associate with one another. After all, sometimes learning can feel anything but comfortable as we find ourselves having to grapple with new ideas, work towards an endless series of deadlines and juggle conflicting pressures. We can also feel like we have very little control in terms of the content we must cover, the assignments we are set and the time we are given to work in.

We may also feel like we have little control over *where* we work and learn, assuming there is a commonly accepted ideal approach which is set in stone. If this 'ideal way' is not effective, we can quickly begin to internalise this as something that is wrong with us rather than the problem being associated with the way of working.

When visualising the 'ideal' environment for study, we often envisage a classroom, library or quiet space at home where we are sat at a brightly lit desk. When thinking of this ideal space, we tend to focus on our physical 'comfort', such as supporting our posture or avoiding straining our eyes. But, in doing so, we can inadvertently overlook our 'cognitive' comfort, which is equally important; our environment can also impact on the way we use our brains to think and learn. This 'ideal' therefore may not be comfy for us all of the time. By focusing on our senses, we can better understand what aspects of our environment distract (and focus!) us, adapting our surroundings to create optimum conditions for us to learn, work and thrive.

In this chapter, we will introduce you to a range of practical strategies to help you to:

- Better **Manage** or **Micro-manage** your environment to increase your sense of control, boost your motivation and remain focused (**Manage your environment** and **Micro-manage your environment**).
- **Move** to a new environment altogether, when possible, in order to harness your 'ideal' conditions for learning.

Don't forget to think about how you can apply all of the different tools you have available to you from the **Welldoing toolkit** when you are considering the strategies in this chapter.

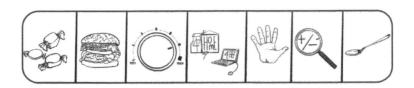

Student voices

'I always felt ashamed of my inability to work effectively in traditional learning spaces. After utilising the **Cognitively comfy learning** strategies and altering my environment to fit what works best for me, my comprehension, focus and retention have drastically improved, and I've never felt more confident in my learning.

Kenna, MSc Management with Marketing, USA '

Check in on your Welldoing... How do your senses affect you?

Before we begin to adapt our environment, it is useful to reflect on the link between our environment and us.

Some of us might feel more (or less) affected by particular senses – we might have a heightened awareness of our surroundings linked to our sense of sight, or get easily distracted by sound. This is different for everyone and can fluctuate depending on many factors. For example, as stress increases, we may become more or less aware of our environment and might start to notice things that we're not normally aware of, such as the ticking of a clock, the tapping of someone's fingers on a keyboard or the brightness of a light. These sensory stressors can make us feel even more stressed, further disconnecting us from our work and interrupting or interfering with our learning (Gallwey, 1974).

Take a moment to reflect on which, if any, of your senses particularly affect you – either reflect on how you feel in the environment you are in right now or think of a time where your awareness of your environment was heightened (or reduced). The sensory wheel (see Figure 2.1) might also help you to consider whether certain senses are more or less heightened for you. Make a note of any sensory issues/indicators you have noticed (feel free to use our **Common-sensory approach to Welldoing template** in **Chapter 10**).

Have you noticed any patterns? The patterns could relate to the senses themselves (e.g. heightened awareness of sounds or smells), where you are or how stressed you are feeling.

Do you notice that:

- clothing labels can feel prickly?
- clothes can feel too tight, such as jeans or your socks?
- certain textures of food are not pleasant?
- certain fabrics feel restrictive or uncomfortable?
- certain textures of surfaces feel funny to touch?

(Continued)

- bright lights or very white lighting can overwhelm you or make you feel anxious?
- certain colours are more noticeable to you?
- a busy environment with lots of movement can be distracting or overwhelming?
- the smell of certain foods can be overwhelming?
- certain sounds are more noticeable to you, such as a ticking clock or someone tapping their pen?

Increasing your awareness of how you are affected by your environment will enable you to better adapt your environment to support comfy learning.

Figure 2.1   The sensory wheel

CAPTION: Use this wheel to help you to consider whether certain senses are more or less heightened for you.

Bear in mind

Use that dial! As explained in the **Welldoing toolkit**, you may find it useful to see how you can apply Welldoing strategies along a continuum. For the **Common sensory approach**, you may find it useful to *reduce* certain sensory triggers which undermine your ability to study. Likewise, you might find it useful to *increase* certain sensory triggers which facilitate your ability to study and use this to actively offset those sensory triggers which are less helpful. As odd as it may seem, sometimes *adding* a distraction can have the reverse effect and actually help us to focus more. A carefully chosen and controlled version of something that normally distracts us can be used to offset other distractions.

Manage your environment

The following cognitively comfy learning **Manage your environment** strategies enable you to personalise and adapt your environment, harnessing your senses to provide you with greater control of your surroundings. The strategies have been grouped under the five senses so you can easily locate those that might work best for you; however, don't forget that you can **Pick and mix**, **Develop your combo** and **Turn up (or down!) the dial** for many of the strategies for your different senses.

Touch

Snug learning

Depending on the type of work you are doing, Snug learning can be a powerful way of freeing up your thinking. Think of it as cushioning for the brain! If working at a desk, could you try putting on slippers or thick slipper socks, or cocoon yourself by wrapping up in a blanket or dressing gown whilst you work? You might find working on a comfy chair or even in bed helps to ground and focus your learning.

Turn up (or down) the heat

Sometimes temperature can affect our ability to work. Could changing the temperature of the room or of your immediate surroundings help you to focus? You might like to try opening a window to adjust the room temperature. If you like the Snug learning strategy above you could try placing a hot water bottle or heated wheat pack on your lap, or tumble dry a blanket and wrap up in it whilst you work.

Dress for success

If the feeling of your clothes sometimes distracts you from study, don't be afraid to alter or change them. Maybe your jumper is made of a material that feels very itchy so you could switch to a softer piece of clothing which feels much more comfortable. A label might be irritating your skin so you might cut it out and remove that distraction. If your shirt feels too tight, could you put on a loose-fitting hoodie instead?

Increase the pressure

Whilst not an obvious thing to think about, some of us may be affected by weight or pressure and could harness this to boost focus. This could be in the form of a weighted blanket, certain clothes which feel heavier or even weighted wrist bands which help to ground you.

Don't sit still

We often think of learning as something that happens most when we are stationary, but we don't necessarily have to be still to focus our brains and boost our capacity to work. Sometimes standing, walking, jogging or driving can actually boost our capacity for thinking and generating new ideas (Oppezzo and Schwartz, 2014). Could you walk and talk to boost your thinking? Could you record your ideas using the voice recorder on your phone or take a small notebook with you to jot down thoughts?

Tools of the (learning) trade

The very feel of the tools we use for learning can directly shape our ability to work. If you're struggling to capture your ideas on the page, something as simple as changing your pen can be effective – different pens can have a very different 'feel' in terms of their weight, how they feel to hold and how they interact with the page. Likewise, if you're working on paper, the texture and even the weight of the paper can influence your ability to engage – try changing your paper to see if this helps you to engage with your work more easily. If you're working on a screen, using a mouse or keyboard that is right for you could also make your learning more comfy – one mouse or keyboard can feel very different from another, and this varies from person to person.

Furry friends

We might spend time with our pets as a way of relaxing, but our furry friends may actually be able to boost our learning potential as well. Having a pet close by to stroke and snuggle can provide you with company and ground you whilst you work (although as I write this my kitten is now blocking my view and sitting on the keys... note this strategy doesn't always go to plan!).

Pause for thought

Can you think of any other touch-related strategies that might work for you?

Sight

Light bulb moment

We often think of light in practical terms of being able to see what we are doing. But light can also be used to boost our focus and help us achieve those lightbulb moments of learning. Could you adapt the lighting in your working space to better spark your thinking? Consider whether natural or artificial light might help. Do you have a preference for a main light or softer lamp light? As well as the brightness, the actual colour of the light itself is worth considering; do you work best with a white or yellow hue? Could you alter the brightness of your screen to see if this boosts your Comfy learning?

Student voices

 I've come to realise how vital being **Cognitively comfy** is for my ability to function, let alone learn or produce work. Prior to taking this approach, I very much believed I had to learn to work in certain ways. Since realising that I can control some sensory input, I can engage more readily with tasks and I'm more effective with them. Since leaving education, I've successfully used this approach in all areas of my life and it's been hugely effective. Lava lamps are the 'life-hack' I recommend to everyone!

Katie, PhD, UK

Life isn't black and white

Colour can be a fantastic learning tool but can also be a huge distraction if the colours don't work for us. A document of black text on a pure white background, digitally or on paper, might be distracting in itself, potentially resulting in you focusing on the format of the document, rather than its contents. You could try changing the text colour to help you to read and process the words more easily. You could also change the colour of the paper or text background – have a play with colour combinations and colour contrasts to see what works for you.

Walls of distraction/focus

If our working environment is visually very busy, then this can distract us – there might be something constantly at the edge of our vision that keeps fighting for our attention. Can you temporarily take down any posters or things that keep catching your eye and distracting you? Or cover them up – for example, put a sheet over a busy bookshelf to 'neutralise' that space. Would decluttering your work space or moving things around in your working area reduce distractions? Alternatively, busy walls might help boost your focus, motivate or inspire you, depending on your preference. The key is to shape your surroundings in a way that supports your own version of Comfy learning.

Find something to set your sights on!

Whilst some people find background movement (such as out of a window or on a screen) visually distracting, some people can find that this visual movement (particularly if it is repetitive) offers a focus which boosts their thinking and focus. Why not try using a moving screen saver or moving image on a TV such as a flickering fire or waves? Can you focus on any movements outside of the window, such as passing traffic or the movement of a tree in the wind? You could also focus on something that isn't moving, such as the horizon or an object in the distance.

Pause for thought

Can you think of any other sight-related strategies that might work for you?

Smell

The sweet smell of success

Our sense of smell is an incredibly evocative sense and one which we often overlook, particularly when it comes to learning. We might be able to recall scents that are very distracting (like the smell of school lunches!) but we can also use scent as a powerful medium to boost our learning focus. Our experience of scent can be very personal – one smell might enhance focus for one person but not another. Could you try lighting a scented candle or an incense stick which has your favourite scent? Could you replicate certain scents you might associate with particular environments, such as the seaside or the garden?

A clean slate

Some of us associate the smell of cleaning products and clean clothes with a sense of newness and fresh beginnings, helping to boost and refocus us. Could you clean your study space to invigorate your sense of smell, or wear freshly laundered clothes and breathe in the scent?

Smells like home

Sometimes recreating smells that remind us of an environment we feel safe in can help to ground us and put us in the right frame of mind for study.

Pause for thought

Can you think of any other smell-related strategies that might work for you?

Sound

Tune in

Sound is an incredibly powerful and emotive sense which we can harness to boost motivation and productivity. Not only can we play with the *level* of noise that best suits us, we can also adapt the *type* of sound. Different types of sound could be harnessed to boost different types of thinking or tasks, depending on whether we need to motivate ourselves, focus intensely on something or spark our creative thinking. Which type and level of sound work well for you? This might differ depending on the type of task you are doing.

Background noise

Sometimes background noise, such as a busy coffee shop or the sound of passing traffic, can help us to focus on our work. If you can't move to your ideal setting with the right background noise, can you recreate this where you are? Would the sound of background chatter, running water or passing traffic help to create the right ambience for studying?

Musical motivation

Rather than thinking purely in terms of turning your music on or off, try to match different types of songs, artists or genres to the type of study you need to engage with or the kind of thinking you want to promote. Do lyrics help you to focus or distract you? Could you build a study playlist (or several) so that you can suit your music to your mood?

White noise

White noise such as a fan whirring, a washing machine running or radio static can be used to drown out or camouflage other background noises that are distracting you.

Sounds good to me!

It might be that you prefer to hear speaking in the background whilst you work, rather than a voice being accompanied by music. For example, try playing an audiobook that you know really well already, or the audio from a well-loved film or play.

The sound of silence

If you feel the need to remove as much sound as possible to avoid being distracted, you could consider using headphones or ear mufflers as a way of dampening the noisy world around you.

Pause for thought

Can you think of any other sound-related strategies that might work for you?

Taste

Food for thought

Food and drink are a great way to not only keep motivated but also to build in a reward for working. When using food and drink, think about how it motivates you rather than simply thinking about your favourite foods or tastes. Play with your taste buds and see if certain tastes or sensations boost your thinking. Is it the warmth of the cup of tea or the salty taste of crisps that really hits the spot? Do you really like something sour like lemons to wake you up and get you going again?

Study snacking

The temptation is to go and grab our favourite foods or sweet treats. Put together a shopping list of study snacks – get creative. Varying our snacks can also keep us motivated as it brings something new to each study period, reinvigorating your motivation. Also reflect on whether you really can eat and work simultaneously or whether it distracts your focus and it might instead be better to separate these activities.

Take a fresh breath

Sometimes feeling fresh can help us to get into the zone of working. Could you try brushing your teeth before you start work? This fresh feeling, as well as the association of cleaning our teeth at the start of the day, can help us get into the right mindset to start a task.

Suck it and see

Sucking and chewing are powerful reflexes which can be used to calm us down and help to displace tension (think of football managers chewing on the side of the pitch!).

Could you try chewing gum or sucking on a sweet or an ice cube whilst working to see if it helps with your focus?

Pause for thought

Can you think of any other taste-related strategies that might work for you?

Micro-manage your environment

In the **Manage your environment** section, we considered how we can use knowledge of how we are affected by our environment to either change it or adapt it in order to boost our learning potential and make sure we are comfortable to learn. However, we will also experience times when it is not possible for us to alter or adapt our environment easily. We may find ourselves in a busy environment that we cannot shape or alter (such as a classroom or lecture theatre). Or we may find that we are working with others and our working environment preferences do not match or complement one another. There will also be times when we feel that we have heightened stress but have very little or no control over our environment, such as when doing a presentation or attending an interview.

How to tweak your environment when you have limited control

The following section will provide you with practical strategies for managing your environment when you may feel less able to directly control or influence your surroundings. We refer to this as **Micro-managing** and this strategy generally involves making smaller (but impactful) adaptions which can increase our sense of control.

When considering **Micro-managing**, you might like to think about the **Manage your environment** strategies and which were most relevant to you. Here are a small selection of **Micro-managing** strategies to get you started. They have also been categorised under the five senses so you can easily locate those that might work best for you. It's also really important to remember that **Micro-managing** is very personal and there is scope to be creative, so do keep adding to the list as you find extra strategies that work for you.

Touch

- Change your clothing or footwear. Maybe wear a thick scarf, or wear thicker socks?
- Use a fidget toy, or fiddle with a watch, jewellery or a hairband around your wrist.
- Doodle on a page.
- Make mini-movements of your foot under the desk or try stretching if you can't move.
- Push your toes into the floor.
- Rub the fabric of your sleeve.

Taste

- Sip water from a bottle – you could even try flavoured water and choose a flavour that works for you, or add a squeeze of lemon or lime.
- If possible, bring a hot drink of your choice in a take-away cup.
- If possible, chew gum or suck boiled sweets.
- You can even get chewable pen toppers!

Smell

- Wear perfume, aftershave or a scented hand cream.
- Use a specific washing powder or fabric softener.

Sight

- Change position in a room so that the light is not as bright or in your face.
- Watch a fire image on a laptop.
- Wear glasses with reduced glare or sunglasses.

Sound

- Use headphones rather than speakers to access sounds that help you.
- Wear headphones to block out noise.

Pause for thought

Can you think of any other ways to micro-manage your environment?

Move

It is important to remember that your needs change and an environment that works for you for a specific activity at a certain time may not work all of the time.

Moving on

If you cannot **Manage** or **Micro-manage** your environment because you're in a shared space, can you physically take yourself away from the distraction by **Moving on** to a new space and place where the distractions are reduced, or to a place where you can take back control of managing or micro-managing your environment again? Reflecting and being honest with yourself about what is working, and especially what is no longer working, gives you the control needed to help you to remain focused and productive.

Feeling ~~out of~~ in place

By reflecting on your environment and how this impacts on your ability to study, you will gradually build up a better sense of what your ideal work space looks like. Reflecting on both the type and level of sensory input you like can help you to identify the working environments that are right for you. The **Move** approach might encourage you to head off to the library or a coffee shop and build a sense of routine associated with where you study. Wherever you move, don't be afraid to choose a space that best suits your needs.

The authors' approach to Welldoing

Thinking about our cognitive comfort has transformed the way we all work. We have learnt to adapt our surroundings depending on the task at hand and how we are feeling. As an example, this chapter was largely written either in bed or with the aid of a soft blanket and hot water bottle as well as the company of kittens or a dog snuggled at our feet!

My blank canvas

Use this space to make a note of strategies you think could be useful to help you make your learning comfy. Remember to **Pick and mix, Develop your combo** and **Turn up (or down) the dial**, so that you can personalise an approach that works for you.

Don't forget that you may find some of your favourite strategies from this chapter help you to apply **Welldoing4home** and **Welldoing4work**. Similarly, can any of the strategies you have selected be applied at a **Micro and macro** level? Could the strategies in this chapter be used to help you to save much needed **Spoons?** Remember that you can also make a note of strategies from other chapters in this space – think outside the box and consider how other strategies from elsewhere in the book might make your learning more comfy.

Key take aways

- You have more control over your learning environment than you might think – you don't have to study in the stereotypically quiet and organised environment.

- Harness your five senses to adapt your environment to maximise your study potential.

- **Manage** or **Micro-manage** your existing environment, or **Move** to a new one, fluidly adapting to maximise your chances of focusing in on your study effectively.

Further resources

- To help you to make the most of our Cognitively comfy learning strategies, see **Template 1: The common sensory approach to Welldoing** in **Chapter 10**.

- There are lots of websites that address the role of our senses in terms of comfort. For example, this blog post from the University and Colleges Admissions Service (UCAS) outlines how your surroundings affect how you study: www.ucas.com/connect/blogs/how-your-surroundings-affect-way-you-study And this page on the Autism Speaks website: www.autismspeaks.org/sensory-issues

- Note that many websites addressing our senses and capacity to learn are targeted at supporting people diagnosed with autism. However, we believe that the strategies shared on such sites go beyond supporting just those with an autism diagnosis and instead can be beneficial for everyone to a greater or lesser degree.

Time and task savvy learning

Adapt and flex your schedule for efficient learning

Is this chapter for me?

- Do you tend to overestimate how much you would like to do in the time you have available and then feel frustrated when you don't achieve this?

- Do you feel wedded to your original plans, even if they don't seem to be helping you to make progress?

- Do you sometimes find it hard to connect and get started with tasks, feeling like you are wasting time?

Time and task savvy learning: The big picture

One of the biggest challenges with time management is managing something that feels anything but constant, manageable and predictable; it can often feel as though time is managing us rather than us managing time! Time can feel like it drags, that it is running away with us, or that there just isn't enough of it. In other words, time can actually feel very *un*predictable.

We might try to take control of time by filling in a diary, or creating a calendar or time-table, organising and dividing our time into discrete chunks allocated for different purposes. Whilst this seems like a sensible place to start, this individual time plan can quickly become an idealised version of how we would like to use our own time, based on 'a good day' when we are working at our best and most efficient. As a result, a few days in, despite our good intentions, our over-ambitious schedule has fallen by the wayside. This undermines our wellbeing and leaves us feeling guilty, frustrated, and with a lack of control over our own time (Aeon, Faber and Panaccio, 2021).

Tasks can be more complex and demanding than we initially realise, or can consist of many more steps than we had first thought. We may also struggle to connect with the tasks we have set ourselves to complete as we are just not in the mood to do that particular task. In spite of this, we still often fall into the trap of forcing ourselves to try to complete a large and often unrealistic number of tasks. When we don't succeed, our motivation and productivity then nose dive as tasks start to stack up and we feel out of control. A disconnect commonly exists between the targets we set ourselves when planning tasks and what we can actually achieve in a healthy and sustainable way.

In this chapter, we will introduce you to a range of practical strategies to help you to:

- Develop effective time management habits which are tailored to your changing needs and circumstances (**Time savvy learning**).
- Manage and progress all those tasks that are demanding your time and energy in a way which is flexible and sustainable (**Task savvy learning**).

Don't forget to think about how you can apply all of the different tools you have available to you from the **Welldoing toolkit** when you are considering the strategies in this chapter.

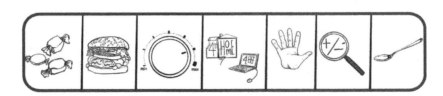

Time savvy learning: Effective and personalised time management

Time savvy learning will equip you with a range of strategies that will help you to plan and manage your time in a way that gives you structure, routine and targets, but is also flexible and responsive to your changing needs. The following strategies can be used to help you to plan a workable, flexible and sustainable timetable or schedule, or to help you reflect more generally about how to effectively manage your time, linked to your changing needs and fluctuating pressures. Your needs can change on a day-to-day, week-to-week or even month-to-month basis. Think about when you may need to approach your time differently and don't be afraid to change your approach to meet your needs (Dierdorff, 2020). The blank timetable template (**Template 2 in Chapter 10**) can be used to help ensure you **Manage your time rather than your time managing you!** Combine this with our time savvy strategies detailed on the following pages. As well as blocking out, chunking and buffering your time, you may also want to consider the other time-based strategies that we share to help you get the most out of your schedule and further increase your flexibility.

Check in on your Welldoing... How time sensitive are you?

It might help you to increase your awareness of how long you spend doing things and become more sensitive to how you use your time. For example, start a task and start the clock at the same time – how long does it take you to finish the task? Alternatively, you might start a timer and see how much of a task you can complete in a specific amount of time, for example 30 minutes. Getting a *rough* idea of how long things *actually* take helps us with planning our time and tasks more successfully. For example, we often think it doesn't take us long to get ready in the morning, or that we don't spend much time responding to emails, but actually it often does. And conversely, we often underestimate how long it takes us to fully review lecture notes or get home after we have attended classes.

Block out your time

An important thing to consider is being realistic about when you don't want to or can't study. This can help you to avoid cramming your study and learning tasks into your schedule and moving or removing all of the other aspects of your life that keep you motivated and inspired, or that you need to do (see **Figure 3.1**). In order to block out your time:

1. **Block out non-negotiable hours/days.** For example, when are you committed to a job, voluntary work, sport training, a hobby or caring responsibilities? Consider whether these might also change week by week or at different times of the year. For example, sport training might only occur during term time.
2. **Block out days and times to suit your own studying preferences.** We don't all study well at the same times of day, nor can some of us work every day of the week. Reflect on how many days you want to base your schedule on (e.g. a seven- or five-day week) depending on what works best for you. Do you want to study in the evenings or early mornings or a mixture throughout the week? Obviously, we can't always choose exactly when we want to study so bear this in mind too.

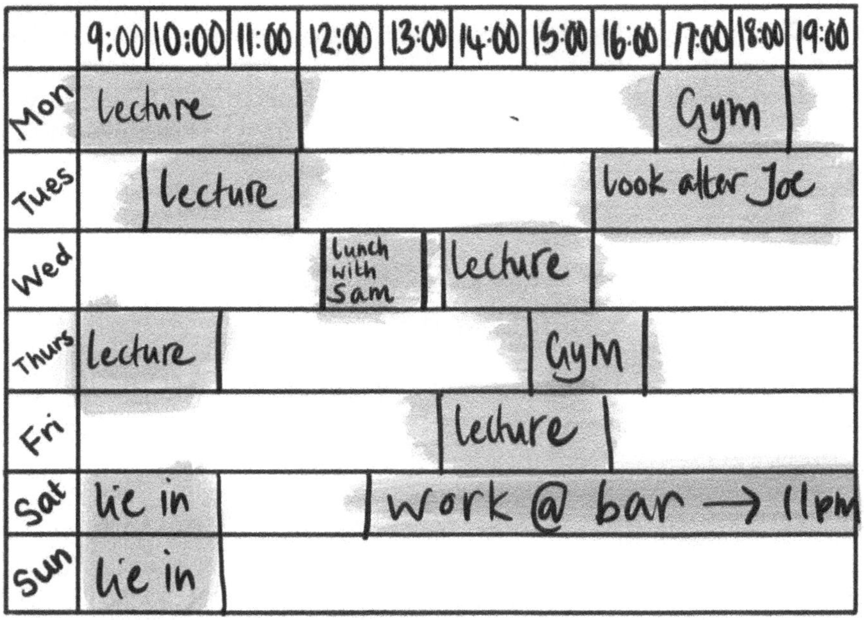

	9:00	10:00	11:00	12:00	13:00	14:00	15:00	16:00	17:00	18:00	19:00
Mon	Lecture								Gym		
Tues		Lecture							look after Joe		
Wed				Lunch with Sam		Lecture					
Thurs	Lecture						Gym				
Fri					Lecture						
Sat	lie in		work @ bar → 11pm								
Sun	lie in										

Figure 3.1   Block out your time

CAPTION: An example timetable of blocked out time.

Buffer your time

When you've blocked out times that are not available for study, it's useful to consider how you might like to use the time that *is* available to you, building flexibility into when you study. Using the **Buffer your time** strategy helps us to avoid that awful feeling of not keeping to the timetable and allows for unexpected events to appear.

This is a really important (but often ignored) aspect of managing time effectively. Perhaps setbacks, social opportunities or deadlines that you couldn't foresee appear, or your mood and motivation wanes one day but goes through the roof the following day. Having buffer time enables you to work more flexibly and provides the opportunity for you to take account of these events, take time back for yourself and still meet your target (see **Figure 3.2**).

1. **Decide roughly how many hours you might want (or need) to study in a given period of time, e.g. one week.** You might, for example, be aiming to complete 15 hours of revision or work on a project in one week. Think about *why* you have this target in mind. Have you worked backwards from a deadline? Have you worked more or fewer hours than this previously and recognise this to be a good balance from experience? Knowing why this is your target can keep you motivated.
2. **Now buffer this time** – take the total number of hours that you want to complete and then (as strange as it may sound!) add additional hours to that total. For example, if you want to complete 16 hours of study, then you could add an extra 25% of this to give 20 hours in total. This would give you an extra four hours of buffer time in the week.

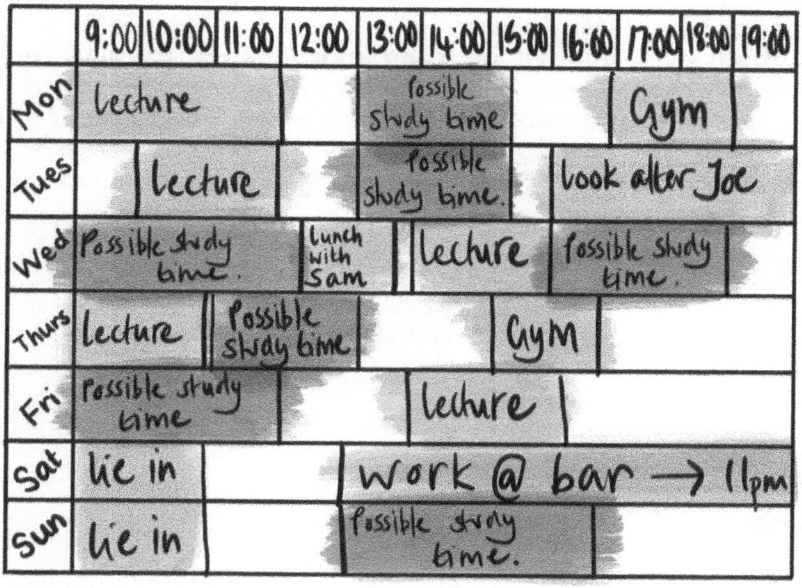

Figure 3.2   Possible study time

CAPTION: An example timetable of blocked out time and buffer time (possible study time).

3. **Schedule the time you want to study** *and* **the buffer time into your calendar or timetable as a total amount.** Including this 'additional' time gives you **Buffer time**, providing greater flexibility in terms of *when* in the week you achieve the target hours and therefore more chance of being able to reach your 16-hour target. When scheduling, you might take into consideration **Blocking time** and **Chunking time** too (see sections above and below).

Chunk your study time

When you are ready to start identifying times for study, another useful strategy is to focus on how you want to chunk your time in terms of what works best for you. For example, there is no point timetabling a six-hour working session if you know that you tend to lose motivation or focus after an hour! Therefore, spend a little time considering whether you prefer working for longer periods or shorter bursts.

1. **Decide what chunk of time you want to have as your default.** It doesn't matter if this changes, but initially it is important to be realistic and build on *your* working preferences and strengths, not those of others or what you might feel is an expected or ideal length of time for working. For example, do you work best in multiple short bursts of activity or longer periods?
2. **Think about what you will be using your time for.** You might like to use your time differently depending on the type of work you are doing. For example, if you are revising, then shorter, focused bursts may be effective, whereas a two-hour block or chunk might be better suited to writing an essay or working on a piece of coursework. Mix and match time blocks to suit your own preferences and the task types that you know that you regularly have to engage with.

Pause for thought

What time chunks would work best for you?

Break time

We often neglect to put in breaks as these might not feel like progress. Scheduling lunch breaks and factoring in some rest time are also things that we often forget to do. Breaks help to refresh us and are important for health reasons too.

Timetable breaks into your schedule and try to stick to these, remembering that breaks will support you to stay focused. It is also possible to set up automatic reminders on your computer that remind you to take breaks for your eyes and for your wrists to avoid repetitive strain injury. Or you could set a timer or an alarm to remind you to take a break.

Bored time

Whilst developing our ability to better plan and manage our time is beneficial, we don't necessarily have to fill up every waking hour with planned activity. Factoring in some downtime and unplanned time can be beneficial, letting your thoughts wander, allowing you time to chill out or enjoy not having to do anything, be anywhere or output anything. It can be really nice when you are normally so busy to just stop and think 'Wow, I literally don't have to do anything now if I don't want to!' And when it's so rare in our busy lives, it can be a real luxury to feel the joy of boredom.

Stealing time

When we think about how to manage and plan our time, it can be really useful to consider all those moments when we might be able to use a bit of time elsewhere, beyond the time that we have planned or mapped out. This can be particularly important for a task like revision, where you might be able to achieve some really short bursts of revision when you are on the move (see **Level 9: Revision on the move** in **Chapter 7**). Can you grab or steal a few moments whilst the kettle boils or whilst waiting for the bus? If you find this strategy useful, you may also want to make a note of these stolen moments (as they will accumulate) so you can get a greater sense of achievement.

Bear in mind

Although this can be a very useful strategy for some, don't feel you have to work in this way and make sure you don't start to fill all those moments that could be used for downtime, which is also very important. If the wait at the bus stop or waiting for the kettle to boil is 'sacred' time that lets your mind wander and provides a much-needed break, savour those moments and don't steal time from them!

Flexi-time

With the best will in the world, sometimes you may find that you struggle to focus and connect with your work, even though you had planned to be studying! There may be times where you need to step away, take a walk or do something completely different. You may need to allow yourself some extra flexibility in terms of maybe starting or finishing later, or having a longer break. There may also be times when you're really in the zone of working but a break is scheduled. Whereas the **Buffer time strategy** helps you to plan in a way that allows greater flexibility in general, this **Flexi-time strategy** provides an extra layer of flexibility and frees you up from feeling that you have to be governed by your pre-planned schedule at all times.

Tweak time

Remember that your initial version of a plan might not be the final version and that any schedule or plan should evolve over time. You may want to adapt your plan regularly, for example on a week-by-week basis, depending on your changing needs and circumstances. Furthermore, if your plan isn't working, for whatever reason, rather than abandoning your schedule or plan completely, revisit the strategies and make small tweaks or adjustments so that your plan evolves to suit your needs.

Task savvy learning: Effective personalised task management

Task savvy learning will equip you with a range of strategies to help you to set realistic targets for managing your tasks, breaking tasks down into manageable steps and increasing your flexibility to move between tasks to maximise your effectiveness and productivity. It will also enable you to work in a way that is sustainable and linked to your changing needs and fluctuating pressures.

Breaking tasks down

Sometimes the nature of a task can feel overwhelming, or it might seem so large that you feel daunted and don't know where to start with it. Additionally, what we initially perceive as one task might actually be made up of a number of smaller pieces.

Breaking large or overwhelming tasks down into bitesize pieces can help us to connect with them and reduce the uncomfortable, overwhelming feeling we initially had when thinking about the task as a whole. For example, rather than listing 'read book' you might break that task down into manageable, bitesize pieces, such as reading one chapter, a page or even a paragraph. Importantly, the bitesize pieces can vary in size, depending on the level you need them to be broken down to, and this can fluctuate, depending on how you feel. There is no limit to how much tasks can be broken down. Rather like a recipe, if you follow one small step at a time this will quickly begin to add up and move you towards your goal.

Pause for thought

Think of a task you have been set or that you set yourself recently and practise breaking it down into smaller, bitesize pieces. Use our **Break it down! How to make tasks more manageable template** in **Chapter 10** (**Template 3**).

Breadth and depth tasks

Not all tasks are created equal! **Depth tasks** require your undivided focus, normally for a relatively long period of time, and they can be quite cognitively demanding. **Breadth tasks**, on the other hand, are ones that do not require as much focus and tend to be less cognitively demanding but they can still take a lot of time, especially when combined. Note that one task that you see as a depth task may be a breadth task for someone else, such as proofreading or designing a presentation. Reflect on your tasks and separate them out based on how much attention and focus they require; those that require complete focus as depth tasks versus breadth tasks, where you don't mind moving from one to the next. Now think about how you will work in a way that allows you to give your undivided attention to the depth tasks, for example switching off email notifications or moving your phone away so that it is out of reach.

Pause for thought

What distractions would you need to remove if you were working on a depth task and how would you remove or reduce them?

Quick win tasks

Some tasks are bigger than others in terms of the amount of time they will take to get done. The bigger tasks can often feel like the harder ones to get into. Have a look at the tasks you need to get done and see if you can identify any that you can quickly and easily complete to get you started and in the zone for working; for example, replying to an email, scheduling a meeting or proofreading a short piece of writing.

Tricky tasks

In the same way that you can identify **Quick win** tasks, it can also be helpful to identify tasks which you find personally challenging. We call these **Tricky tasks**; tasks that, for whatever reason, you may have trouble completing and that seem to present a huge hurdle or challenge for you. They can also be tasks where you might need help or input from someone else. What seems like a tricky task will be different for each person. When combined with a big workload, a tricky task can seem even more challenging. It's important to be realistic and identify tricky tasks because then you can start to see what input you might need to complete the task. Just as you might start with **Quick win** tasks, don't worry if you leave a tricky task until later on in the day once you have gotten into the right mindset. This can also help reduce pressure as you have already made progress with other tasks, freeing your mind up to focus on the tricky task.

Batching tasks

This strategy helps you to get on a roll by grouping tasks in terms of their similarity or type. This could include **Quick win** tasks such as deleting emails, or could include longer or more complex tasks by 'type'. As an example, sometimes we would write this book in this way; we would think about all of the things we needed to do (e.g. formatting, editing and creating content) then in a session we would focus on one of these aspects across sections and chapters.

Use **Template 4: Break it down! How to organise tasks by type** in **Chapter 10** to help you to organise **Breadth** and **Depth tasks**, your **Quick wins**, your **Tricky tasks** and tasks that lend themselves to **Batching**.

Multiple-choice buffering tasks

In an ideal world, you might allocate specific tasks to a specific time, but this approach doesn't actually give you the freedom to do what you're in the mood for and so might not support you to work efficiently and effectively. This can inadvertently lead us into an all-or-nothing mindset where, if we can't successfully connect with the subject or task we have timetabled, then we feel we have not hit the target we set for ourselves. The **Multiple-choice buffering tasks** strategy enables you to factor in choice by allocating two or three tasks to a timeslot, so that when the time comes around you have the flexibility to choose the task that you are in the mood for or feel motivated to tackle.

Bear in mind

Whilst this strategy can be a life-saver and help to boost our productivity, just be mindful of not inadvertently putting off specific topics or tasks repeatedly!

Dabble with tasks

Some days it can be really hard to find a way of connecting with a task. The task schedule ahead of us feels insurmountable and we might feel incapable of achieving what we had set out to achieve initially. Rather than thinking 'I must do some work', use the **Dabble with tasks** strategy. This strategy focuses on how to get into the zone when you can't connect with tasks. Try working on one small bit of one of the scheduled tasks for a few minutes – even if it's not the task you have set yourself to do at that particular time. If this doesn't work, step away and then try dabbling with another task instead. The dabble with tasks strategy can help you to move fluidly from one task to another until you find a way in and connect to a task.

Take it easy!

In a similar way to the **Dabble with tasks** strategy above, some tasks feel much more doable than others. This is very personal and what constitutes an easy or a hard task will be different for everyone. If you struggle to get started with work and find you are a master at procrastinating, try starting with the easiest tasks rather than battling to connect with and complete a task that is far more challenging. Once you have ticked off a few easier tasks (see the ~~To do~~ **Done** strategy on page 45), you may find you have more motivation to have a '**dabble**' with the more tricky tasks that need to be done.

Check in on your Welldoing...
Setting the pace

Everyone's natural pace is different and it is important to recognise this. Ideally, we need to work towards developing a sustainable way of working where we don't leave things to the last minute, but it is also important to reflect on how you naturally like to work as a baseline. Reflecting on our pace when approaching our list of tasks and why we adopt this can help us better understand how we work and plan accordingly to give ourselves the best chance of succeeding.

- Do you tend to leave things to nearer to the deadline? If so, why do you think you do this? Is it because of the adrenaline rush you get as a deadline approaches which consequently enables you to focus?
- Or do you prefer to space out your tasks, as leaving things to the last minute makes you really stressed and therefore unable to focus?
- Perhaps you like to work in short, focused bursts as you know you have a short attention span, for example using a timer to set a specific timeframe in which to work.

When setting your pace, try to be realistic. If you are someone who tends to be a late starter and works in intense bursts to get you over the finish line, it is unlikely that you will change overnight into an early starter who gets the work finished weeks before it is due. The key is to recognise how and *why* you work in the way that you do, to try and harness this and to draw on other strategies to kick start or boost your pace when required.

Making good time: Taking note of your progress

Whilst time and task management often encourages us to think ahead, it is equally important to *look back* and take note of what you have achieved. It can be all too easy to not register how much you have done, instead focusing on the next load of 'to-do' tasks or deadlines you need to work towards. But noting progress is vital as this reminds us to acknowledge our accomplishments and how far we have come. It also boosts our motivation and provides us with a much-needed sense of completion.

As modern life becomes more fast paced and we pile on the expectation in terms of how much we should all achieve, the need to step back and acknowledge what we have done is becoming increasingly important. Recognising that tasks reach completion through incremental steps, no matter how small these steps forward might feel, can help us move beyond simply thinking about tasks as done or not. If you struggle to acknowledge your progress, then try some of the following strategies to help you to actively track your progress. Use our **Taking note of your progress template (Template 5, Chapter 10)** in conjunction with the following strategies.

~~To do~~ Done lists

It can be so easy (and disheartening) to replace one to-do list with another; as soon as we complete something, our minds are already racing ahead thinking about the next set of goals we have to meet or targets we have to achieve. Shifting our focus and producing **Done lists** rather than a traditional to-do list can help us to take note and recognise the progress we are making.

You might also find it useful to keep your Done lists, rather than deleting or throwing them away, so that it provides you with a clear and constant reminder of how you have moved forwards.

Bear in mind

You might like to try combining this approach with the **Breaking it down** technique so that you record smaller steps and mini-targets in order to ensure you see that you are moving forwards. For example, writing 'finished essay' on a done list is very satisfying, but it may be some time till you have the satisfaction of achieving this. Therefore, try writing smaller done tasks, which will all add up to help you meet the overall goal, and will help you to take stock of the progress you are making over time.

Done hours

Don't forget that a done list doesn't just have to include tasks; you may like to record the hours (or minutes) of work you have completed to help see your progress. You may like to keep a tally of the time you have worked so that you can see this is building. If you have been using small bursts of time to help plan your working schedule, you could record these bursts of time so that you can see how they start to mount up.

Progress checker

Rather than fixating on the fact that you haven't yet completed the work required, try and focus instead on how much you have moved forward and know that no matter how small the steps are that you have taken, these ultimately add up and move you forwards towards your goal: believe us, we should know as we have had to use this technique repeatedly to produce this book!

The progress checker lets us move away from the idea that something is either done or not – instead, you measure distance travelled. You can use percentages of colours to note how you have moved forward on a particular task. For example, you may not have finished reading an article, but you could use a percentage to measure what you have achieved so far. In the same way, a traffic light system (red, orange and green) can also be used to show you are making progress and moving in the right direction. Note that this technique can also be combined with the **Breaking it down** approach listed above.

Don't forget that colour can also provide a useful tool to highlight the progress you are measuring. If you have made a timetable, you might like to change the colour of the complete blocks from one colour to another so that you are giving yourself a visual reminder of what you have achieved.

You might also find it helpful to keep a visual map of your progress. This is something you can get creative with and personalise so that it works for you. Maybe you could draw out a road, some footprints, a tree or maybe a spiral – you can add to this every day, so that it gets longer and becomes a visual reminder of the distance travelled. Have a look at the **Taking note of your progress template (Template 5, Chapter 10)**. There are also many apps available to help you check your progress.

Student voices

‘Many of the strategies discussed in this book were explained to me in its infancy, before they were printed for the reader's use. They helped tremendously when learning to understand my anxiety and how to cope with my own expectations. In particular the aid of diagrams such as creating my own 'progress snake' helped me visualise that learning, and indeed its drawbacks, is never linear. This enabled me to remember that whilst education has many ups and downs, you are always moving forward.

Izzy, A levels, UK ’

The authors' approach to Welldoing

With busy lives and multiple commitments to manage, we would often use the **Dabble with tasks** technique to help us get started and get into the zone for writing. We frequently combined this with **Breaking it down**, whenever the task of writing seemed like an insurmountable hurdle. Indeed, this very section was worked on by identifying bite-size chunks of writing we could cope with!

My blank canvas

Use this space to make a note of strategies you think could be
useful to help you make your learning more time and task savvy.

Remember to **Pick and mix**, **Develop your combo** and **Turn up (or down) the dial**, so that you can personalise an approach that works for you.

Don't forget that you may find some of your favourite strategies from this chapter help you to apply **Welldoing4home** and **Welldoing4work**. Similarly, can any of the strategies you have selected be applied at a **Micro and macro** level? Could the strategies in this chapter be used to help you to save **Spoons**, and can you combine any of the strategies with our **Common sensory** approach?

Remember that you can also make a note of strategies from other chapters in this space – think outside the box and consider how other strategies from elsewhere in the book might also help to save you time and energy.

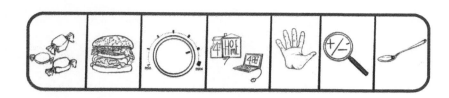

Key take aways

- Plan and manage your time in a way that gives you structure, routine and targets, but is also flexible and responsive to your changing needs.

- Adopting the **Buffering**, **Chunking** and **Blocking time** strategies to plan your time gives you more control over when you study by being realistic and flexible with how you plan your time and tasks.

- When tasks are overwhelming you, set realistic targets by **Breaking tasks down**, **Batching tasks**, looking for **Quick wins** and **Dabbling** to increase the chance that you can maximise your effectiveness at task management and work smartly.

Further resources

- In order to make the most of the **Time and task savvy** strategies, see the following templates in **Chapter 10**:

  - Template 2: Manage your time rather than your time managing you
  - Template 3: Break it down! How to make tasks more manageable
  - Template 4: Break it down! How to organise tasks by type
  - Template 5: Taking note of your progress

- The following blog post gives tips for university students to manage their time and tasks, though the ideas shared within could be used by any student at any level: www.topuniversities.com/blog/7-time-management-tips-students

- Many online timetable generator websites exist. You may find these useful to generate digital versions of your schedule so that you can easily adapt and edit it, depending on your changing needs.

Stress-free learning (well almost!)

Pro-actively manage your varied life demands and reduce unnecessary stress

Is this chapter for me?

- Do you regularly feel like it is impossible to balance the demands of your studies with all the other areas of your life?

- Do you feel like you should be doing everything, and doing it all perfectly and on your own?

- Do you sometimes feel like you have reached your limit, perhaps finding you are constantly worrying or can't sleep, but you also struggle to reset and relax?

Stress-free learning (well almost!): The big picture

We have all experienced pressure associated with our study. This is normal, expected and sometimes necessary; a certain amount of stress can be useful as it can motivate us to reach our learning goals.

But sometimes stress and pressure can mount in the form of multiple upcoming assignment deadlines, high-stakes examinations or covering tricky course material. This can intensify further when we have a strong desire to do well and be the best version of ourselves. And although there is absolutely nothing wrong with aiming high, pushing ourselves and striving to improve, this can also exacerbate the level of stress we experience.

In addition, managing stressful study periods would be much more straightforward if study was the only thing we had to concentrate on. However, we don't study in a vacuum; pressures beyond the classroom can mount as we try to juggle multiple areas of our lives. This can fluctuate from day to day, week to week or even season to season. At times, even things we look forward to, like spending time with friends or focusing on a hobby, can cause unintended additional stress. Achieving the holy grail of a sustainable work–life balance – a perfect equilibrium where we work hard and achieve, as well as finding time to rest, recuperate and take care of ourselves – is often easier said than done!

Whilst it's not possible to remove *all* the stress from learning, we can take action to manage mounting stress and pressure.

In this chapter, we will introduce you to a range of practical strategies to help you to:

- Recognise when and where stress and pressure are rising across the different areas of your life and take active steps to effectively manage this (the **Stress-free learning approach to managing and reducing pressure**).
- Take positive action when balancing the demands of life and learning starts to feel impossible and you feel like you are running on empty (the **Stress-free learning approach to rebooting**).

Don't forget to think about how you can apply all of the different tools you have available to you from the **Welldoing toolkit** when you are considering the strategies in this chapter.

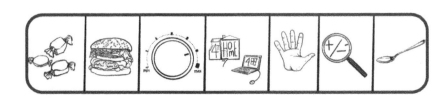

The stress-free learning approach to managing and reducing pressure

As we have mentioned, our study does not take place in a vacuum. The pressure and stress we experience from learning might be made up of different subjects or a number of conflicting deadlines which compete for our attention. Similarly, the pressures associated with life can be multi-faceted, from pressure linked to employment, to keeping on top of day-to-day chores, or managing our finances, and being there for friends and family. We are constantly managing numerous competing demands, which can contribute to mounting stress and an overwhelming sense of imbalance. Recognising how the multiple areas of our lives are interlinked and are interacting in a constant state of flux can help us to understand how to manage the stress we feel.

Check in on your Welldoing...
Saving our spoons (SOS)

Balancing competing pressures and stress feels different for everyone. Our capacity to manage this can also fluctuate; at certain times we feel more able to balance life's daily demands than at others. The concept of using **Spoons** to help us to save energy, work smartly and prioritise was introduced as part of the **Welldoing toolkit** in **Chapter 1** – if you are new to the power of Spoon saving, then take a look at our Welldoing **SOS (Save our spoons)** on page 10.

The metaphor of Spoons provides a tangible tool to help us actively reflect on how much energy is available to us. The metaphor is particularly useful when we are facing increased pressure and stress and we feel that something may have to give! Reflecting on the competing areas of stress in our lives by using Spoons helps us to prioritise those things that are most demanding of our attention at a specific point in time. It can help us to recognise where we might be able to temporarily alleviate pressure in one or more areas and save some much-needed Spoons.

(Continued)

- At this moment in time, are there any areas where you could re-prioritise in order to give your Spoons a boost?

For example, if you have an assessment deadline approaching, you might check in on your Spoons to see where you can potentially reduce or alleviate pressure in another area.

- Could you get a take-away so you don't have to cook?
- Could you leave the washing up until the following day?
- Could you do 15 minutes of exercise instead of your normal 30 minutes?

Actively thinking about and responding to mounting pressures in this way help us to develop flexible habits that enable us to more effectively juggle and balance the various competing aspects of our lives.

Bear in mind

Whilst it is useful to take action to manage pressure and stress by finding opportunities to save Spoons, be mindful to not consistently cut corners in areas of your life that are good for you and are required to keep your life balanced and healthy.

Spoon-saving strategies

The following strategies can be used to actively manage and lower stress, saving your spoons. Also see our **Template 6: Save our Spoons!** in **Chapter 10** to help you make the most of the following strategies.

A helping hand

When life feels particularly full-on or overwhelming, try getting a helping hand from your peers, family or friends. This might include working with others on a specific task or identifying road blocks where someone else may be able to help you move forwards. Could others make you a meal or do your washing (as long as you then return the favour!)? Remember that this is a great way of saving Spoons for the tasks that are demanding our energy and undivided focus, such as exam revision or an approaching deadline.

Student voices

'Understanding the reasons behind my high-stress levels was the first step that has helped me to understand how to manage it, remembering that we cannot resolve everything at once, but to prioritise and break things down into smaller steps. A strategy which I have found particularly helpful was the **saving Spoons** strategy, which has enabled me to reduce the pressure on myself.'

Filip, BSc Architecture, Poland

Prioritising pressures

We may want to achieve every goal we set for ourselves but sometimes we simply can't. It is important to remember that not all tasks are equal. Using a simple letter-based system (ABCDE) or a colour-coded traffic light hierarchy (red, orange, green) can help you to reflect on the level of importance of a given task. For example, do you really need to send that email now or can it wait until the end of the week in order to stagger how you spend your Spoons? If you have received feedback but you don't have the time, energy or motivation to respond to every comment, which ones will help to improve your work the most?

- The **4Ds** of **do, defer, delegate and delete** (Canfield et al., 2013). This can help you to think about tasks in a way that not only considers their importance but also how or when you might like or need to complete them (e.g. immediately, by the end of the week, by the end of the month). This allows you to work out what you need to **do** and what you can **defer** (for the time being at least). You may also be able to identify tasks that you could **delegate** to someone else or **delete** from your to-do list entirely. Importantly, the 4Ds strategy can be just as easily applied to tasks beyond study. Practising this technique on everyday tasks that are not related to study first might also seem less of a risk than testing it out on your study, helping you to build your confidence in deferring, delegating and deleting. Feel free to use our **Prioritising pressures template** in **Chapter 10 (Template 7)** to help you 'do, defer, delegate and delete' your tasks when they start to mount up.

Pause for thought

Try applying the **4Ds** to some of the tasks you have lined up at the moment.

If something's worth doing, it's (sometimes) worth doing less well!

When time is running out or we simply have too many things to juggle, we might need to re-evaluate the expectations we place on ourselves. It may not feel comfortable but it might be important to ask yourself '*When is "good" good enough?*' We all experience bad days and on days like this it is important to be kind to yourself, considering what is the minimum you have to achieve that day. You may decide to do fewer things (and do them to a standard you would like to maintain) or do all of the things you have set out to do but perhaps at a slightly lower (more sustainable) level. This aspect of Welldoing encourages us to fluctuate expectations of ourselves so that we can sustain effective working habits and take care of our wellbeing, allowing us to save Spoons.

Bear in mind

This can be a very hard skill to develop and lowering the expectation you place on yourself may not come naturally. If this is the case, try working with others to make it a reality; sometimes asking permission from someone else can help validate the notion that removing some pressure is a good or necessary thing to do.

Turbo boosting

Although we should work towards a good work–life balance overall, it is sometimes necessary for us to go into overdrive in one area of our life for fixed periods of time or for specific goals. This is a normal and sometimes necessary part of study. Busy times, with multiple deadlines and simultaneous demands from different areas of our lives, can be particularly draining. When this happens, the key is to take note and adapt your approach by drawing on strategies to enable you to manage this increased pressure by reducing your expectations in other areas.

Bear in mind

Remember that this is a temporary turbo boost. Whilst it is healthy and useful to actively take control and fluctuate pressures, and this strategy can help for short periods, it is important to remember to reset.

Smart study

Smart study involves adapting the *way* in which you approach learning, which can impact on the time and energy you spend on your studies, helping to ensure that learning becomes as efficient as possible. For example, could you boost your revision efficiency and reduce pressure by using the **Revision Elevator (Chapter 7)**? Could you use our **PIES: Recipe for a tasty paragraph** in **Chapter 6** for building your paragraphs and therefore save energy and time later by having to do less editing on your essay structure? Remember Smart study equals saved Spoons!

Under promise and over deliver

Sometimes we can develop habits which appear to be helpful and useful to us, but which can also inadvertently increase others' expectations of us. If you find it hard to say no and you worry about letting others down, then the following strategies will help you to find realistic and sustainable ways of supporting or meeting the needs of others, whilst not leading to burnout. Get ready to under promise and over deliver!

Deadlines and targets window

Rather than specifying an exact time and date when you will get something to someone, try giving yourself a slightly larger window of time. For example, rather than saying 'I'll get that to you by the end of the day' maybe suggest that you will get it to them within the next couple of days. This will naturally start to build in some flexibility.

Email delay

If you are always tempted to reply to an email or text straight away, could you challenge yourself to delay this a little bit? This can take the pressure off and help you to avoid others coming to expect an instant reply, or you feeling that you have always previously replied quickly so should continue to do so.

Work in progress...

If you are working with others and need to send them your contributions, rather than always feeling that you need to send a finished version of something, try using the percentages model of progress or colour-code your work using the traffic light system. This can be a way of giving yourself permission to send something that is not perfected, polished or completed.

Saying no

The more we say yes, the more others grow to expect this of us (and often we subconsciously expect this of ourselves too). Learning to say no can present a real challenge and is not likely to be something we can do overnight. Start small and first practise doing this in areas of your life that feel less high-risk. For example, you might not feel able to say no to a teacher or your boss, but might find it easier to say no to a friend.

Pause for thought

Are there any events coming up that you feel that you *should* go to but don't really *want* to go to? Perhaps use this as a chance to start to practise building up the confidence to say no.

The stress-free learning approach to rebooting

We will all experience times in our life when we feel we are running on empty or stretched to breaking point. Short intensive bursts at working and living at full capacity are manageable, but it can sometimes feel that we are living under a permanent state of high stress. At this point, we might be encouraged by others to 'take a break' or step off the treadmill; deep down we also know ourselves that it is important to recuperate, replenishing our Spoons and aiming to restore balance to our lives. However, we can also feel that stepping back is counter-intuitive to achieving our goals and making progress, experiencing a tension between having lots on but also needing to take a break. This tension can further elevate our stress levels and actually even start to affect our ability to relax. We might find ourselves in a situation where we know we need to spend time resting and relaxing, however our busy and stressed minds are unable to switch off, preventing us from winding down or even from sleeping. We have included a specific template in **Chapter 10** so that you can capture those strategies that you may need to go to when the pressure is on and you need to give your own Welldoing an extra boost (see **Template 23: Take your Welldoing up a level**).

Welldoing approach to worry management

Worry is a natural part of the learning process, linked to uncertainty, change, unpredictability and things being beyond our control. Worry could also be viewed as an exaggerated version of the very same skill set that helps us to succeed in our studies, a heightened or unregulated version of our ability to think, critique, analyse and evaluate.

Therefore, some level of worry is expected and can be seen as part of our learning journey. However, when we feel overwhelmed by pressure or stress and are unable to effectively control or manage our worries, we can go into over-thinking overdrive, turning our ability to critique, analyse and evaluate in on ourselves. Being caught in this vicious cycle can become exhausting.

If you are a natural worrier, then you're unlikely to completely get rid of this part of your personality, but you can learn to work with it. The **Welldoing approach to worry management** will help you to better understand why you are prone to worry, how to break this cycle and harness and manage your worries in a way that helps you to problem-solve and move forward. Don't forget to refer to our **Worry work-out template (Template 8)** in **Chapter 10** to make the most of the strategies.

Check in on your Welldoing...
Your worry patterns/triggers

It can be useful to try to understand if there is any underlying pattern to your worries.

For example, is there a yearly pattern to your worries linked to the course or the structure of the academic year with peaks of stress (e.g. exams, social pressures associated with a particular time of year)? Are there any other triggers (e.g. hormonal cycle, sleep struggles, social, personal)?

Once we are able to better predict when worry might strike and in what form worries might occur, we can then better anticipate any triggers and pressure points and be more prepared for them. By better understanding the underlying causes of our worries, we can adopt strategies that help us to actively manage them.

Bitesize approach to worries

If we try to tackle a worry as one isolated thing, we might find we become frustrated that we can't find a way of overcoming the worry. Instead, try breaking worries down to help solve them. As an example, if we identified we were worried about doing a presentation this could be several smaller worries, such as the fear of forgetting what we need to say, fear of people looking at us, fear of not being able to answer a question if put on the spot or the fear of being seen as an imposter. Breaking down the worry into its constituent elements helps us to start to find focused solutions that target specific aspects of one larger worry. This strategy can be particularly useful when combined with the **Worry writing** method below.

Pause for thought

Can you think of any worries that you currently have that you can break down further into bitesize pieces to better understand them?

Worry writing

Writing down your worries can be cathartic. Capturing them on the page can put some distance between you and your worries and enable you to look at them more objectively. Some people like to journal their worries and find free-form writing can help them to work through their worries as the thoughts spill out onto the page. Sometimes a more structured form of **Worry writing** can also be useful, where the worry is more systematically broken down and worked through on the page (see the **Bitesize approach to worries** pages 57 and 58).

Parking worries

If you are a natural worrier, then acknowledging your worries rather than ignoring them can be really important. Acknowledge and register your worry, but try and get into the habit of parking it by either making a mental note or capturing it on paper as a reminder. This will enable you to identify the worry, whilst storing it away to worry about later, at a more convenient time. You might like to then combine this with the **Worry time** strategy (see below) so that you actively ear-mark a time when you can come back to your worry and deal with it then.

Worry time

Sometimes factoring in a specific or designated time and space in your diary, maybe weekly or daily, can help us to manage worries in an effective way. Worries can then be 'stored' (see **Parking worries** on the previous page) and then revisited when time and space allow. You may find it helpful to limit the time you're allowed to focus on the worry (e.g. ten minutes) so that you can realistically mull it over or unpick it without getting caught up or stuck on the worry (Farrand et al., 2019). If the worry feels that it is still very real and not yet ready to be filed away, then you could revisit it again at the next Worry time.

A worry a day

If your brain naturally flits from one worry to another, it can be useful to try and pri-oritise your worries, as strange as this may sound! You might find it useful to identify a worry of the week, or worry of the day, which you allow yourself to worry about whilst parking the other worries for later. What's the most important thing to worry about now? Remember that what is important to one person may be different to another so prioritise the worries which are causing the greatest hurdle for you.

Diminishing worries

When trying to deal with a specific worry, it can be useful to think about how that worry might become less overwhelming over time. Ask yourself, will I still be worrying about this in a day, in a week, in a month or in a year? This can be a useful reminder that although a worry can feel significant and overwhelming in that moment, worries often naturally reduce over time. A worry has a limited life cycle. Reminding yourself of this can help to lessen the impact of a worry, even when it is at its peak.

Worry clouds

Many of our worries are transient, and come and go, rather than being fixed and permanent. Some people find that actively visualising their worries and seeing them floating and drifting away like a cloud into the distance, until they are no longer vis-ible, is a useful way of reminding themselves of the temporary nature of many of our worries.

Pause for thought

Give the worry clouds strategy a try yourself right now!

Shape-shifting worries

Sometimes we can feel that as soon as we have solved or mastered one worry, another comes along. When this happens, it can seem that one worry has simply been replaced with a seemingly unrelated worry; one worry morphs into another. However, although not immediately obvious, there may be an underlying pattern which links these worries together. If you look at your worries collectively rather than in isolation, are there any underpinning patterns that start to emerge? Are your individual worries linked to an overarching desire of not wanting to let people down, or are the worries linked to trying to be the best version of yourself at all times? Understanding our worries in this way can help us to better understand where our worries come from and what our worry-related triggers are.

A worry shared is a worry halved

Try talking through your worries with a friend or trusted person. Often people may have the same worries and so it can feel like a relief to vocalise our worries and find out others have the same ones too so we're not alone. Just voicing our worries out loud can also help us to gain a bit of distance and perspective, enabling us to see a way forward.

Harnessing worries

Anticipation of an event or situation which is causing us to worry can often be worse than the actual thing itself. It is quite common to feel an increased sense of apprehension as we get nearer to the source of our worry, such as when an exam or a presentation approaches. It can be helpful to acknowledge this worry and try to view it as something that can actually be harnessed so that we can perform or rise to the challenge. An adrenaline rush can feel uncomfortable but recognising that it can also help to boost motivation and focus is important. After you have done the thing you are worried about, don't forget to take time to reward yourself for facing the worry.

Bear in mind

If you feel your experience of anxiety can be paralysing when trying to prepare for a presentation, then you may also find it useful to look at the strategies to help you thrive at presenting in **Chapter 8**.

Worry work-out

A build-up of worry or stress is often linked to a build-up of adrenaline. This strategy is about using movement to displace built-up stress and anxiety. Physical movement can be used to get rid of adrenaline – try dancing, jumping or shaking your limbs. It can be surprising how quickly your worries can reduce and you can gain a new sense of perspective by physically shaking the worry out! If you are somewhere where you feel you can't move or this would not be appropriate, then even little movements such as tapping your foot or using a fiddle toy might help to displace some of your nervous energy.

The Common sensory approach to worry

In the **Cognitively comfy learning** chapter (**Chapter 2**), we explore how you can use your environment and senses to boost learning. In the same way, we can use this approach when worry is consuming us to re-ground ourselves and connect with the world around us. A stimulus from the physical environment can help to break our thinking and, in doing so, disconnect us from our worries. Try taking a deep breath and feel your feet pushing into the floor. A simple counting exercise or focusing on an object can also help to anchor you. Sometimes an assault on the senses, such as music or movement, can distract your brain and shut down the worry.

Welldoing approach to sleep survival

We are often reminded of the importance of good sleep hygiene habits, such as going to bed at the same time each night and not going on our mobile phones before bed time. But sometimes, in spite of establishing good sleep hygiene, our sleep can still go awry; it can be a frustrating and scary feeling if suddenly we can't sleep, or if our normal go-to sleeping solutions no longer seem to work.

It is important for each of us to develop good sleep hygiene habits, however these habits can sometimes create unintentional added pressure where we strive for the perfect sleep, which may not always be possible. This anxiety can make it worse – we know we should be sleeping but we just can't stop worrying about what knock-on impact this is going to have on our productivity the next day. These thoughts can spiral, and this can in turn make it even more difficult to switch off and sleep. We believe the key to successful sleep is to establish good sleep hygiene habits *and* have a set of sleep survival strategies we can turn to when needed. Use our **Sleep survival template**, in conjunction with the strategies themselves, if you feel your sleep has gone awry (**Template 9, Chapter 10**).

Check in on your Welldoing...
What's my sleep norm?

We all have a different sleep default; some of us sleep for eight hours a night, some might function on lots less than this. Also, sometimes, we have a bad night for absolutely no reason at all – we may have had a great day or not be feeling particularly worried about anything, but our sleep can still be wobbly.

What's *your* sleep norm?

Be honest and realistic so that you can aim for your own personalised version of what a good night's sleep looks like for you. Remember that we are aiming for good sleep habits and patterns over a period of time and the odd bad night's sleep is nothing to lose sleep over!

Wide awake with worry

When you can't sleep, it is worth remembering that this is often a natural result or product of something else that is worrying or bothering us. Sometimes this can be easy to identify, such as increased nerves before an interview or exam, but other times it can be something we might need to spend a bit more time unpicking. Be kind to yourself and try to lower your expectations in terms of getting your ideal sleep in this situation. If you are worrying about things, no matter how seemingly trivial, have a look at the **Welldoing approach to worry management** strategies earlier in this chapter.

Redefine sleep time as rest time

If you are really not able to sleep, then redefining this as 'rest time' can help to reduce that vicious cycle of worry about not sleeping. Instead of fixating on sleep (or lack of), focus instead on getting comfortable and trying to rest.

Sleep buffers

Giving yourself longer in bed or setting the alarm for later (when possible) in the morning can also help to reduce the pressure of worrying about lack of time left to sleep, particularly when you have to wake up by a certain time. If possible, giving yourself a sleep buffer in this way can help you to reduce the pressure associated with time.

Hyper-focus

The example of counting sheep is often used to illustrate how focusing our brain can be a useful approach to helping us to drift off. Some people like to count, some might list countries or objects – this encourages hyper-focus and helps to reduce the noise of lots of competing thoughts.

Scattered thoughts

This is almost the opposite of the **Hyper-focus** strategy (see above). Try to replicate the process your brain goes through when we go to sleep, so rather than focusing on one thing or using a highly structured approach such as listing or naming, you might like to encourage your thoughts to flit from one unrelated thing to another. This can actually help to disconnect or scatter our thoughts.

Stop the clock!

Whilst technology can be helpful and reassuring and help us to track sleep progress, don't overlook the need to step away from it if fixating on sleep data is making you feel more worried or stressed about your sleep patterns. Too much attention paid to sleep data might make monitoring and measuring our sleep become yet another area of our lives that we try to set targets for.

Pause for thought

If you gather data about your sleep, do you think it is aiding you to sleep better?

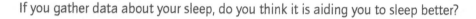

Acknowledge your achievements

If you do sleep one night and start to break the cycle then acknowledge this. But if your sleep goes awry again, remind yourself that it is likely to be temporary. It will return and by trying out different strategies, you can help yourself get back to a better sleep routine more quickly.

Get out of bed

As odd as it may sound, our bed can become a symbol of safety, sanctuary, the ultimate comfy space, but when we are struggling to sleep, the bed itself can become a constant reminder of our inability to drop off to sleep in the space that is specifically designed for that. Therefore, although not a long-term solution, removing yourself from your bed can actually reduce this 'pressure' to go to sleep. Could you try sleeping somewhere else, such as in a different room, on the sofa, in a different bed or even on the floor?

Pause for thought

Where else could you temporarily try sleeping, other than your bed?

The common sensory approach to sleep

We have already introduced the common sensory approach to helping you to switch off and offset your worries; using our senses can also be a really powerful way of helping us to overcome challenges we may be facing with sleep. Playing with our surroundings and making small adaptations drawing on our senses can provide us with a powerful toolkit for surviving difficulties with sleep.

Weighting for sleep...

A weighted or heavy blanket or a heavier duvet can help to make us feel more grounded. The increased pressure on our bodies can help the body to override the mind and help it to switch off.

Hit the pillow

Sometimes propping ourselves up with an extra pillow or changing the height of our pillows can help. You might find flipping your pillow, removing it completely or sleeping 'upside down' (with your head where your feet would normally be) helps.

Grounding yourself

Focus on your own breathing and the sensation of breath moving into and out of your body to distract the mind. Smoothing the bedding or rubbing your feet together can help to ground you. Sleeping with a pet can also really help when we are struggling to sleep – listening to the sound of their breathing and stroking their soft fur can help to ground you.

The sound of silence?

Sometimes when we can't sleep, a background noise can be calming and provide something for our brain to focus on. Try different types of 'sound' such as an audiobook, a podcast, some music or maybe white noise as the type of sound needs to be right depending on our personal needs.

A breath of fresh air

Opening the window and feeling fresh air on our faces can aid our ability to sleep. Listening to the sounds outside can also give our brain a focus.

Light sleeper

It may be that your normal go-to for sleep, such as having the room pitch black, may not be helpful to you if you are struggling to sleep. You may find it helpful to adapt the lighting. Consider whether having darkness or soft lighting, such as the door ajar so you can see light in the hallway, helps. Or maybe consider leaving the curtains open.

Pause for thought

How could you apply the common sensory approach to sleep to your own sleep?

Welldoing approach to active relaxing

As we all lead busy lives, it is easy to fall into the habit of equating success and achievement with productivity and output. We may feel like we're wasting time if we're not always being 'productive'. However, taking a step back to reboot and recharge is vital for retaining productivity. This can create space for your brain and body to recover from all the hard work, which then helps to boost capacity for thinking and learning when you do return to studying. We can also spontaneously have some of our best ideas when we are not working and our brains have freedom to think.

However, sometimes we end up in a halfway state where, although we are taking time out with the aim of relaxing (e.g. having a bath, going for a walk), we actually feel unable to fully switch off or wind down. In this case, try the following Welldoing active relaxation strategies to help you to actively boost your ability to switch off, unwind and recuperate. Don't forget to use our **Active relaxing template** if helpful (**Template 10, Chapter 10**).

Target setting

In a world where we are constantly encouraged to work towards targets, it can be very hard to get off the treadmill and take time out. If you find it hard to stop or feel guilty when you relax then you could set targets linked to things that help you to relax. This then enables us to directly harness our desire to work towards targets and use this to support our ability to switch off and take time out. You might find it helpful to actually schedule relaxation time into your week or set targets that you can then tick off such as reading a chapter, watching an episode of a series or walking a particular distance. Using targets in this way might seem counter-intuitive, but if you find it really hard to switch off and relax, then this can help you to see value in taking time out.

Bear in mind

Whilst a target-driven approach can help us to relax and work towards goals that directly support our wellbeing, remember that the target is there to encourage you to do nice things, rather than as something to measure ourselves against. We don't want to turn relaxing into another job that is driven by goals and pressure!

Get busy relaxing

It may sound like a contradiction to get busy in order to relax, but sometimes by actively engaging in a hobby we can switch off more than when we are trying to relax and unwind but without a clear focus or purpose. If you find it hard to switch off, try using an activity to focus your mind. This could be colouring, reading, playing an instrument, watching a film... the possibilities are endless but the aim is to identify that sweet spot where you engage in an activity which requires your attention and focus at a level which helps you recuperate rather than leaving you feeling drained.

Clocking off

As life becomes more busy and demanding, it can become harder and harder to carve out time and justify Clocking off, especially when there are always endless jobs we could be doing. Allowing yourself designated time to switch off and planning this into your week can help to make relaxing become more of a habit.

Pause for thought

To what extent do you allow yourself time to Clock off?

Common sensory approach to active relaxing

As discussed in the **Cognitively comfy learning** chapter, adapting our environment can directly impact on our ability to relax. Here are a few examples to start you off...

- If you find that you sometimes eat without thinking, focus on tasting your food and hold it in your mouth for a little longer than normal.
- Use headphones to immerse yourself in music, or use white noise or noise-cancelling headphones to drown out all other sounds.
- Use a camera to help you 'zoom in' and focus on specific things in your environment to help you reconnect. This will help you see the world around you through fresh eyes and help to focus the brain on specific points, rather than being overwhelmed by or ignoring your surroundings.

- If you find nature relaxing then try finding a green space, slow down and take time to notice the world around you.
- Different scents can be used to shape and alter our mood and may help boost your ability to relax and switch off.

Pause for thought

How could you apply the common sensory approach to active relaxing in your own life?

The authors' approach to Welldoing

We all have a tendency for perfectionism and don't like to let people down, so we have had to use this chapter a lot to make life manageable and develop sustainable ways of working. Karen has had to think about **Saving spoons** and how to use the sleep strategies to help with the arrival of her baby (who likes to be up quite a bit in the night!), and Abby has to repeatedly remind herself to prioritise tasks and remember that it is OK to do things less well! Loti uses a lot of the **Active relaxing** strategies so that she makes the most of her time off from work.

Key take aways

- Actively manage and lower stress by paying attention to how you can save your Spoons by using strategies such as a **Helping hand**, prioritising pressures by using the **4Ds** and **Turbo boosting** for a short period of time.

- If you find it hard to say no and worry about others' views of you, try **Under promise and over deliver** so that you build in some flexibility and reduce the pressure, such as using the **Email delay** and **Deadlines and target windows** strategies.

- When you're running on empty, focus in on the **Welldoing approach to sleep survival, worry management** and **active relaxing**. Try strategies such as **Parking your worries** or scheduling **Worry time**, redefining sleep as **Rest time** or planning **Sleep buffers**, and using **Target setting** to support active relaxing.

- You can also help yourself to reboot by connecting with your senses to find effective ways to actively relax, as well as sleep and manage your worries through the **Common sensory** approach.

My blank canvas

Use this space to make a note of strategies you think could be  useful to help you make your learning as stress-free as possible.

Remember to **Pick and mix**, **Develop your combo** and **Turn up (or down) the dial**, so that you can personalise an approach that works for you.

Don't forget that you may find some of your favourite strategies from this chapter help you to apply **Welldoing4home** and **Welldoing4work**. Similarly, can any of the strategies you have selected be applied at a **Micro and macro** level? Could the strategies in this chapter be used to help you to save **Spoons**, and can you combine any of the strategies with our **Common sensory** approach?

Remember that you can also make a note of strategies from other chapters in this space – think outside the box and consider how other strategies from elsewhere in the book might also help to make your learning stress-free!

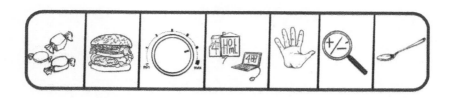

Further resources

- In order to make the most of the **Stress-free learning** strategies, see the following templates in **Chapter 10:**
  - o   Template 6: Save our Spoons!
  - o   Template 7: Prioritising pressures
  - o   Template 8: Worry work-out
  - o   Template 9: Sleep survival
  - o   Template 10: Active relaxing

- As we said in the **Big picture** for this chapter, we believe in complementing good sleep hygiene with the Welldoing approach to sleep survival. The Sleep Foundation has written a good overview of sleep hygiene which you could use in conjunction with the Welldoing approach shared in this chapter: www.sleepfoundation.org/sleep-hygiene

- Mindfulness apps also exist to help you to actively relax. For example, the HeadSpace app is very popular.

- Take a look at this cognitive behavioural therapy evidence-based approach to help manage generalised anxiety disorder (GAD) from the University of Exeter https://cedar.exeter.ac.uk/media/universityofexeter/schoolofpsychology/cedar/documents/liiapt/coverimages/2018CLES039_CEDAR_Managing_Your_Worries_(BW).pdf. Although it is targeted at those diagnosed with GAD, it contains effective strategies that could be helpful to all.

- If you want to learn more about cognitive behavioural therapy, take a look at this webpage: www.healthline.com/health/cognitive-behavioral-therapy

- Medical professionals – as discussed in the Prologue, this book is not a therapeutic book. Its aim is to act as a preventative toolkit, so we strongly encourage you to reach out for professional and medical help should you find yourself in a position where you are chronically stressed, struggling to sleep or worrying.

Reader's and writer's block

Adapt how you interact with the page to get started with reading and writing tasks

Is this chapter for me?

- Do you find that you feel overwhelmed when faced with a blank page and this stops you getting started on a task?

- Do you struggle to organise thoughts, ideas and notes, or capture these efficiently and in a meaningful way?

- Would you like to improve your reading efficiency so that you can work smarter rather than harder?

Reader's and writer's block: The big picture

The term writer's block has become a commonly used phrase to describe the difficulties many writers experience when they can't get their words to flow and cement them successfully on the page. We can all experience this frustrating state where the gap between the blank page and the 'thinking' occurring in our brains can feel like a huge gulf which feels impossible to breach. We tend not to give the space on a page much thought, but how we interact with this space can shape our ability to think, learn and write. It is possible to overcome this fear of the blank page and instead harness it so that it becomes a powerful thinking space instead, an extension of your brain where you can learn to organise your thinking and communicate this effectively to others.

The opposite of writer's block is also very common, where the words on the page, no matter how hard we try, simply won't bridge the gap and cement themselves successfully in our brains! Just as some of us fear the blank page, we might also experience fear of the written page. We call this reader's block. Just as we can learn to control and utilise the blank page to better support our writing, we can also find ways of controlling how we interact with the page when we are reading.

It can be really helpful to see reading and writing as two sides of the same coin, rather than separate aspects of learning which require different skills. In this chapter, we will explore practical strategies to enable you to interact with the page in a way that can help you to overcome both reader's and writer's block and boost your thinking and learning potential by developing smart reading, writing and learning habits.

In this chapter, we will give you the tools to:

- Harness the blank page in front of you to overcome writer's block (**Fear of the blank page**).

- Utilise the space on a page to boost your ability to think, process new ideas and organise your thoughts in a way that works for you (**Thinking spaces**).

- Take effective notes in a way that supports your thinking (**Taking note of how we take notes**).

- Overcome reader's block and interact with the written page in a way that supports your thinking and learning (**Overcoming reader's block**).

- Boost your reading speed and reading efficiency (**Zoom reading**).

Don't forget to think about how you can apply all of the different tools you have available to you from the **Welldoing toolkit** when you are considering the strategies in this chapter.

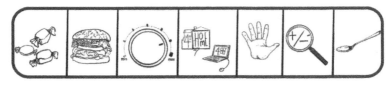

Fear of the blank page

The worst part of working on an assignment or a project is often getting started. Being confronted with a blank space that we know we need to fill can not only cause frustration and demotivate us, but can also impact on us emotionally, leading to self-doubt or feelings of imposter syndrome. We may feel completely paralysed either by the sheer size and scale of the task we have to complete or by the fact that the blank page represents so many endless possibilities!

We often don't think about the blank space, whether it is physical or virtual, but actually spending some time reflecting on how we use and interact with this space can help us to better capture our ideas and connect with the planning process. This can help us to effectively organise our ideas and feel like we are making progress. Just as our environment or surroundings can affect how we feel and our ability to learn, so too can the actual page in front of us. Therefore, the way we interact with a blank page is central to our Welldoing: things like the colour of the page or how we divide up the space to make it less daunting can help us to get started.

Have a look at the following Welldoing strategies to help you to overcome the fear of the blank page. Also refer to our **Fear of the blank page template** in **Chapter 10 (Template 11)**.

Every bit helps

The first thing you write on a page is often not your best and most fluent work, however this is totally OK as it gets you started and immediately removes the blank page. Every word or phrase, image or doodle helps move away from this daunting blank space. It can be very tempting to cross out or delete the first things you write, but unfortunately that will keep returning you to a blank page.

Divide and conquer!

Rather than seeing the page as a single, blank and overwhelming space, it may help you to divide up the page. You could use lines, boxes or different shapes to create a series of smaller safer spaces to work in. If working on paper, you may find it useful initially to fold or cut up the paper so that you limit the size of the space you are working in. Take a look at **Thinking spaces** too which comes a little later in this chapter.

A picture is worth a thousand words

Why not try using images on the page to help start off your thinking? This can help you to start the process of recording your ideas on the page without getting caught up with finding the right words.

Make the page mucky!

Sometimes a pristine page can be really off-putting. A mug mark, a doodle or a creased page might help to make the page feel like you own it and offset that temptation to keep the page pristine.

Write as you speak

Sometimes it can be hard to commit words to paper so let speaking guide your writing. Distance yourself from the actual act of writing and the pressure that this can generate and think about speaking your words to free you up. If you speak your ideas out loud first, you can then capture them in written words or images as needed.

Match your mood

Whether working on screen or on a physical page, changing the style, size and colour of the font or the background may help you to better connect with the space in front of you. Consider whether it is helpful to theme your background using a software package, for example Microsoft PowerPoint.

Colour coding

This can be a very powerful way of enabling you to get some ideas down on the page without being tempted to make the writing perfect or hit the delete button. A traffic light system of **red**, **orange** and **green** can be useful. This helps to break the cycle of feeling the need to write down finished, fully perfected sentences. We can use **red** to capture initial ideas without feeling the need to polish it there and then knowing that we need to return to these words. **Orange** can be used to indicate that something we have written is good or has potential but still needs a bit of refining.

Green can be used to indicate that our writing is good to go. You might find that you have a whole chunk of writing that is red or just individual words or parts of sentences. The idea is to use colour flexibly to free up your thinking and writing.

Student voices

'The colour coding tip under **fear of the blank page** has been really helpful to overcome self-criticism in writing. It really helps to block out the work which is good to go and the text that needs to be further worked upon. This helped me with an upcoming essay to complete despite the self-criticism and produce a good essay.

Harshita, BA Psychology, India '

Quotation marks

Try starting with the words of someone else. Start with a quotation or a prompt and work from there if you are struggling to find your own words. However, make sure you don't fall into the trap of plagiarism by passing off someone else's words as your own – remember to use references to support your work. See our **As easy as pie(s) section** in **Chapter 6** to help you with this.

Printed and virtual pages

Even if you need to produce a digital version of your work, you may actually find it useful to move between the digital page and a physical piece of paper. Sometimes, bringing together our ideas or planning is easier to carry out on a physical page, whereas the editing and tidying can be easier to manage when working from a digital copy. So don't forget to try and move between the printed and the virtual page as you develop your writing.

Dot dot dot

Use this strategy if you can't think of the right word or how to finish a sentence or idea. Instead of getting stuck on trying to come up with the right word or phrase, use a simple '...' to indicate a gap and come back to this later when you feel fresh.

Thinking spaces

Sometimes we can work perfectly well and achieve our goals without having done any formal planning and we find it is easy to think of ideas, evidence these and arrange them on the page without having to break down this process. However, the bigger the piece of work, the more demanding the assignment or the more tired and overwhelmed we might be feeling, the harder it becomes to address all of these features of planning simultaneously. Developing our ability to control the spaces that we use for thinking and planning can remove huge amounts of pressure, thus easing the feeling of being overwhelmed and providing us with a much clearer plan of action.

Furthermore, in the **Cognitively comfy learning** chapter we explored how fundamental our environment can be in making us physically and cognitively comfortable and thus ready to learn. Our environment can shape and influence our very ability to focus on a task; it can be used to increase our motivation, boost concentration and focus and make the process of study much more efficient. We can apply this very same thinking to the page in front of us, whether this is physical or digital.

Pause for thought

Take a look at the space on the page in front of you, whether paper or digital, where you tend to work – this will ultimately be the space where your great ideas come to fruition, the space where you express yourself and the space where you work out how best to convey your ideas to others. Yet, ironically, we don't routinely give the space we use for thinking much thought. If we pay a little bit more attention to our thinking spaces and how we engage with them, we can learn to shape, manage and control them to boost our cognition and support us to work in a way that meets our needs and harnesses our potential.

The mind map

The mind map has become the most commonly used go-to approach when getting started with a piece of work and trying to capture our words or ideas. The mind map can be brilliant for helping you to see the shape of a subject; it can help you to link one idea to another and get a sense of the big picture (see **Figure 5.1**). The mind map can work particularly well when you're getting started with a piece of work or if you are struggling to link different concepts or ideas together.

Figure 5.1 Thinking spaces – The mind map
CAPTION: Example mind map.

Using colour coding or sketching images or diagrams can also really support the mind map method for planning and capturing ideas – this is another example of developing a combo of Welldoing strategies for greater impact and efficiency. Colour can be used to group ideas and highlight links, which may in fact expose patterns or themes that exist within our ideas. Images and diagrams can also help us to make links between ideas and see how knowledge fits together. See our **Thinking spaces – The mind map template** in **Chapter 10 (Template 12)**.

Bear in mind

Mind maps may lead to information overload. Some of us can experience analysis paralysis as we can see too many ideas, make too many links or see endless possible combinations for sorting and organising the information we are generating. If mind maps send your brain into a meltdown or into panic mode then explore some of the other approaches we have outlined below as these provide more structured and broken-down ways of collating your ideas, planning and writing.

Thinking inside the box: Tables

The table might not be the most obvious go-to when planning or starting to write a large or demanding assignment, yet it is particularly useful. Tables can help us to break down the steps involved in writing, significantly reducing information overload and analysis paralysis (see Figure 5.2).

Paragraph	Point	Information	Explain	So what?
1.				
2.				
3.				
4.				
5.				

Figure 5.2   Thinking inside the box
CAPTION: Example table.

The table above contains a number of columns and rows. In this example, the columns have been used to help us to remember to include the **PIES: Recipe for a tasty paragraph** in **Chapter 6**; each row can be developed into a paragraph in its own right. By breaking down our thinking in this way, we focus solely on each specific and individual step of the planning process, without the fear that we will miss out a key step. We may temporarily focus in on capturing our ideas, or trying to arrange and sequence these ideas in a way that makes sense to the reader, to make each step of the process feel manageable, but by using the table we are reassured that we won't miss out any essential ingredients. See our **Thinking spaces – Thinking inside the box template** in **Chapter 10 (Template 13)**.

Bear in mind

The **Thinking inside the box: Tables** strategy is most useful when we are faced with a daunting, complex and overwhelming writing task. Sometimes the table method can feel too prescriptive, too controlled and can make the writing and thinking process feel too broken down. If this is the case then try another Welldoing Thinking Spaces strategy.

Bullet points

A good compromise or combined approach which draws on elements of both the table method and mind mapping is the bullet point strategy. Bullet points, when combined with **PIES: Recipe for a tasty paragraph** in **Chapter 6**, can provide the same focus as a table and break the task down into manageable chunks, without feeling too prescriptive or too controlled. Using some colour-coded bullet points such as **PIES** can help us to stay on track and organise our ideas.

Bear in mind

If you are using a recipe, such as **PIES**, to help you to build your paragraphs, remember the Welldoing approach and adapt the formula you are using so it best suits the type of writing you are trying to produce.

Sticky notes

Sometimes we can find that we don't have any issues with generating ideas; we could easily fill a page with our thoughts and do so quickly. It is of course not a bad thing to have lots of ideas, but sometimes when we have so many ideas we might not know how best to order and sequence these. The challenge is recognising the overall shape of the *narrative* we wish to produce. Sticky notes can provide a really powerful strategy for helping us to arrange and organise our ideas. When we capture ideas on a page in the form of a mind map, table or bullet points, we can very quickly feel like the words are becoming fixed or cemented on the page, particularly when this page feels very tangible like a piece of paper; we can worry that if we move one sentence, idea or piece of information then our whole narrative will begin to crumble.

Capturing our ideas on sticky notes provides us with greater flexibility and a sense of fluidity; the notes can be moved, rearranged and re-ordered until we feel that we have organised our thoughts in the most logical way possible. We can apply the **Welldoing toolkit** easily to this strategy; the Sticky notes strategy can be used at a **macro** level to organise key ideas for paragraphs or sections of a piece of work you're producing, but equally it could be used on a **micro** level to build a really tricky paragraph where you know which sentences you would like to include but cannot quite determine how the sentences should be arranged in order to convey your message as effectively as possible.

Washing line

Like the **Sticky notes** strategy, the **Washing line** provides you with even greater flexibility and makes the organisational part of thinking and writing more easy to control. The Washing line strategy is exactly as it sounds: set up a piece of string suspended in the air and then hang your individual ideas (captured on separate pieces of paper) on the line. When using this strategy, it helps us to see that nothing is set in stone and the pieces of paper can be moved and rearranged quickly and flexibly into a linear order. Something about the physical movement of the pieces of paper can boost our cognition and confidence at carrying out what can sometimes be a very complex and overwhelming task. Remember that the Washing line can be used at a **macro** level for mapping out an assignment with lots of different sections, or at a **micro** level for simply tackling a few sentences that you just can't get to grips with.

Erase and rewind

When trying to evolve our ideas on a page, we may find it helpful to use a digital page or a mini-whiteboard. It tends to be easier to erase, move and update our ideas and understanding on these types of pages compared to when using traditional pen and paper (though you could of course use a pencil that can be erased!). This can free us up from the anxiety of making a mistake that feels permanent when written in ink on a piece of paper, allowing us more freedom to try it out and develop the page.

Bear in mind

Be aware of losing important ideas when erasing or updating ideas without any trail. Take a look at **The ideas freezer** strategy in **Chapter 6** to avoid this happening.

Keeping up the colour

We have referred to the importance of colour throughout this book. Colour is one of the most powerful yet simple tools for helping to boost our thinking and give us greater control over the work we are producing. Colour can be used to help us organise ideas, such as in a mind map. It can be useful to help us spot patterns or identify themes or anomalies in the information we are gathering. It can be used to help us to ensure that we capture the secret ingredients required for a strong paragraph or it can be used to help us proofread and polish our writing. Therefore, when thinking about which **Thinking space** to use for a particular task you are working on, don't forget to combine this with a good dose of colour coding.

Student voices

' I find a whiteboard is a useful tool when formulating my answers. Firstly, as someone who finds visual aids helpful for their learning, any diagrams and workings out are large scale which is always helpful, and secondly it encourages a more relaxed and fluid thought process. I am able to write or draw confidently knowing that any incorrect parts can be simply erased and amendments quickly made, without committing anything to paper. In this way, I think it helps reduce some of the anxiety of getting the answer wrong. '

Will, BSc Sport and Exercise Science, UK

Taking note of how we take notes: Strategies for effective note-taking

Many students worry about note-taking, especially when trying to do this in a time-pressured setting such as a fast-paced lesson or lecture. The stress of 'missing' a vital piece of information or not being able to keep up with the teacher and other students can lead to us trying to write word-for-word what is being said or what is displayed on the board or the screen. As a result, the power of note-taking for supporting learning is reduced (Morehead et al., 2019); the task becomes focused on reproducing information rather than effectively processing, making sense of and storing it in our brains.

Learning to efficiently take notes in a way that will be most beneficial for you can take the stress factor out of this tricky task and transform the way you learn. It can save much-needed time and energy when it comes to exploring a new subject or memorising it for use in an assessment. Vitally, when we take notes in a way that works for us, we harness this as a learning tool that helps us to unpick and make sense of new materials, as well as organise it in a way that makes sense to us. Use our **Note-taking template** in **Chapter 10** to help you get started (**Template 14**).

Don't forget that note-taking is a skill which we use in multiple contexts. We can take notes in response to a lecture or presentation, when reading a textbook, when making revision guides and when we are involved in meetings or group work.

Bear in mind

Remember that whilst we might not always default to using the most effective study skills, there is something very comforting and familiar about what we already know and our established ways of working. We encourage you to explore new ways of enhancing your note-taking, but do this in a way that is comfortable and at a pace that is manageable. For example, if you are concerned about falling behind when making lecture notes and need to feel confident that you have not missed anything, then practise a new note-taking strategy when the stakes are not as high, such as when making your own notes at home or outside of the busy lecture environment, where you may feel less rushed and under pressure.

Linear notes

This is the most commonly used form of note-taking and one that students frequently default to when under pressure. Linear notes definitely have their place and are particularly useful when trying to capture or make sense of material that follows a specific order in terms of process or narrative. One of the challenges with this form of note-taking, however, is making sure that we don't just copy everything that we are hearing or seeing. Note-taking should aid our thinking and cognitive processing, so although this form of notes is popular, consider whether you could adapt it to better allow you to capture the material efficiently *and* support your understanding.

For example, consider:

- Reducing the amount you write by focusing on capturing key words and concepts, rather than sentences.
- Using a form of shorthand. There may be key shorthand terms that already exist in your subject, or you may like to make up your own. This might include shortened or abbreviated forms of words (e.g. info (information), rxn (reaction), C21 (21st century)), acronyms (PCR, AfL) or symbols such as an upwards arrow to represent 'increase', chemical elements ('Fe' instead of iron), -> for 'therefore'.

Bear in mind

Some students like to write notes in full and can feel disconnected or lost if they don't do this. The important thing is to think about what works for you and practise a new approach over time and in a way that is comfortable for you. Don't feel that you need to fully shorten and reduce your notes overnight.

Pictorial notes

We often associate images or drawings with learning activities we engaged with when we were younger, and this is one of the many strategies we can leave behind or overlook when we move on to further or higher study. Yet, as we have mentioned previously, a well-chosen image or diagram can be a very useful tool to help us process, organise, store and recall information. Pictorial notes can involve using simple doodles, images or diagrams interspersed with written words to cement our learning and boost memory. One of the big benefits of pictorial note-taking is that it can really help us to 'arrange' new information in a way that makes sense to us. For example, making linear notes can lead to linear learning where we process the ideas in the order in which they have been presented to us by the teacher or text-book. Pictorial forms of note-taking, particularly when combined with words, can help us to reorganise ideas in an order that suits our brains, helping us to better link ideas and see the big picture.

Remember that this is also another example of how a great strategy for one specific study-related skill can also help you in multiple areas of your life. Notes in pictorial form may help you with revision, when presenting to others or when remembering key things you want to memorise for an interview.

Digital versus freehand

For written note-taking, you could write using pen and paper or you could record your notes digitally by typing. Some people find that they are quicker at capturing ideas by typing and this reassures them that they won't miss any key concepts. Some people find that when writing using pen and paper, the movement of their hand across the page and the tangible 'reality' of the notes help them to remember and make sense of the material. Consider which is the best approach for you – and this may vary from topic to topic, or day to day, depending on how you are feeling.

Student voices

' I like to note-take using a digital pen sometimes because I know I can write faster than I can type, and I like to add diagrams or drawings to help my under-standing later.

Molly, BSc Medical Biosciences, UK '

Audio notes

We might assume that notes have to be made in written form, but just as pictures or diagrams may help us to boost the effectiveness of our note-taking, so too can the use of audio. Depending on your preference, you may also find it useful to talk through your notes with someone else, or to record these in the form of audio or video, so you start to build your own resources to return to when you need them.

Note the colour

Colour can be a great tool when making effective notes and something we have high-lighted throughout the book as a valuable transferable learning tool. Remember that colour can be used to help us to make sense of information, see patterns, identify key ideas or alert us to something we need to go back to or take note of. Colour can indeed make our notes look nicer, but remember that its greatest function is as an organisational tool to boost our thinking, learning and memorising. Use colour to support learning rather than as a decorative tool.

Interactive notes

This strategy helps you take control of the notes themselves and think about what you are capturing. It is commonly used when making linear notes. Use the margin on a page or create your own so that you mark out a separate, clear and empty space alongside the area of the page which you will be using to make notes. As you are making your notes, use this space as an opportunity to note how you are feeling about the notes you are taking. For example, you might like to use this space to note when you have come across an important concept or idea that you would like to revisit. Or you might like to make a note when you have covered something that you don't understand and need to read up on further. You could also use this as a way of highlighting where you got lost or fell behind. Making a note of this in the margin space can free us up as we have mentally noted that we need to catch up on something, but once noted can move on and try and reconnect with the content.

Spaced out notes!

This strategy supports the other note-taking approaches explored here. We have already mentioned the importance of space on a page to help to separate out materials and naturally 'chunk' information, but it also provides us with the 'space' to think and process the knowledge itself. If space is something that helps you to feel less overwhelmed and more in control of your learning, then try and harness this when making notes. Use space around important concepts or ideas. Space also enables us to go back and add to or refine our notes; just as our thinking is organic and develops, so too can our notes. See **Fear of the blank page** earlier in this chapter for further suggestions of how you can make the most of the blank page when making your notes work for you.

Overcoming reader's block

Just as we can all experience writer's block when attempting to communicate our ideas in writing, it is also not uncommon to experience *reader's block*; instead of being fearful of the blank page, we are overwhelmed by the written page and the sheer enormity of carrying out the reading task we are faced with (Mehelin, 2022). Just as there are many ways to overcome the fear of the blank page and get started with writing, there are also strategies we can use to help make the task of reading more manageable and effective.

Before we begin exploring some strategies to ease the reading process, it is useful to make the distinction between the skill set we use when we are *learning to read* and the skill set we use when we are instead *reading to learn* as part of our studies. Think back to some of your earliest memories of reading as a child. As children, when we start developing our literacy skills to support effective reading, every word on the page is treated as equally weighted. This might sound like a strange statement, but if you are working to unpick a sentence such as the 'cat sat on the mat', each word must be decoded in turn in order for us to process and understand what the writer is trying to communicate. As we get older and more experienced, our reading speed starts to increase and our confidence at decoding increasingly complex sentences improves.

But no matter how quick our reading speed or ability to decode the letter symbols and sounds in front of us, at some point we will all be faced with the very real challenge of ploughing our way through large quantities of reading materials that need to be digested in a relatively short space of time. The sheer volume of words that need translating into something of meaning can seem insurmountable. Furthermore, if we found the mechanics of reading harder to master when we were younger, we can doubt our ability to engage with long and complex articles and texts.

To save our sanity at this point, it is worth remembering that when *reading to learn* for our studies, we are actually employing a different skill set than the one we initially mastered when we were learning to read. Of course, decoding individual words, syllables and letter sounds is still of fundamental importance but in this next section we'll focus on a range of Welldoing strategies to boost your reading speed, improve your confidence at skimming and scanning reading materials, and develop all-important reading comprehension skills. These strategies will help you to efficiently assimilate and process the ideas that you are reading and give you greater control over the often laborious process of wading through a long reading list. It is worth noting that these are not skills that we can master overnight or over the course of one assignment, but something we need to work on and revisit over a prolonged period to fully embed this into our default way of working.

Deciding when a resource simply isn't for you

All of us have had an experience where we have picked up a book or read an article and found that we just cannot connect with it; for whatever reason, we find that we simply cannot make sense of the ideas nor get to grips with the writer's communication style.

When we are faced with this situation, it can be very common for us to think this problem is ours alone. However, it is important to remember that not every resource will be equally accessible and usable for each of us: reading is a highly personal experience and not everything we read will be written in a way that we like, let alone can process and make use of. Despite this, many of us persevere, tirelessly attempting to wade through text that is simply not going in and sticking in our heads. It can be really useful to remember that sometimes it is OK to step away from a textbook or resource and replace this with an alternative information source, if possible. This is particularly useful if you are struggling to get to grips with a new concept or idea; switching to another text provides a new opportunity to engage with the material in a way that is more manageable and makes sense to us.

Break it down

When faced with a particularly long or complex article or book, it can be helpful to break down the task of reading into manageable chunks. Start by seeing if you can identify the amount that you need to read. Whether this is a chapter, a whole section or a paragraph – even a few lines. Quantifying the amount of reading you need to do in this way might seem counter-intuitive, yet having a finite amount of reading to work towards provides a useful starting point for us to then break this down further into manageable chunks. For example, if you are faced with reading through 50 pages of complex text, you might like to chunk this figure into smaller sections that you will tackle one at a time, such as five pages. This same strategy can also be applied to paragraphs or even sentences if the reading task is particularly cumbersome or overwhelming. Having a clear start and end point in this way can help us to set a reading-related goal which feels less daunting and is more achievable.

A similar but alternative approach is to set a timer for a short period, such as 15 minutes, and read until the timer goes off. This breaks the big, overwhelming task into short, manageable bursts, helping us to make progress despite the overall task seeming huge initially.

Dabble at reading

You might also like to combine the **Break it down** strategy on the previous page with the **Dabble strategy**, as explored in **Chapter 3**. If your reader's block is a real challenge, try and have a dabble with your reading and read small amounts in order to give yourself multiple opportunities to connect with the task at hand.

Don't look back too soon

Sometimes when we watch a film, a scene may not make sense immediately and we have to carry on watching for a little while in order to fully comprehend it. We can apply this to reading as well. When you are struggling to understand a sentence or paragraph, you might find you get stuck in a loop, re-reading the same sentence or passage without feeling able to move on to the next bit of text as you haven't understood it completely. If this happens, challenge yourself to try and move forwards and see if the next bit of text helps you to better make sense of what you have just read. This can take a bit of confidence and practice so don't push yourself completely out of your comfort zone – do this in a way that you are comfortable with, maybe just encouraging yourself to read on, even if only by a few words or sentences. Then take stock and look back to see if the tricky text now makes more sense. Often you will find that it does!

Common sensory approach to reading: Move, manage and micro-manage

We have already explored the importance of our environment in shaping and harnessing our ability to think and learn in **Chapter 2** on **Cognitively comfy learning**. In that chapter we introduce the importance of moving from one environment to another or managing and micro-managing the environment we find ourselves in. We can apply the same strategies when approaching reading tasks: remember that in **Cognitively comfy learning** we talked about the importance of cognitive comfort rather than just considering physical comfort. This is really important when reading.

Making adaptations to our environment or even the text itself can help to boost motivation and concentration when reading in a way that is comfortable for you.

Move: We may find that certain environments are more conducive to reading than others. Some of us, if we have the luxury of being able, might find it helpful to **Move** to an environment that better enables us to connect with the reading materials, whether this is in the form of a library, coffee shop, outdoors or in the comfort of our own bed.

Manage: It is not always possible to move locations so think about how you can **Manage** your immediate environment to boost your reading potential. This might include adapting lighting, heating or many other variable factors which affect our senses. Likewise, you might also consider using software so that you can listen to text being read aloud or instead try to engage predominantly with podcasts or videos if you find these resources easier to connect and engage with.

Micro-manage: Just as we can't always **Move** environment, we are not always able to **Manage** our immediate surroundings. This is where the **Micro-manage** strategies are particularly useful. This could include changing from a digital to a physical page (or vice versa), altering colour background, text size and font or using colour overlays to make the process of reading more manageable. Remember that reading, like any study or learning-related task, doesn't happen in a vacuum or in isolation. By increasing our awareness of how our senses and our surroundings shape our cognitive functioning, we can take greater control of those aspects of study that we find most challenging. **Micro-managing** enables us to make small, often subtle tweaks which have impact. This could include using a fiddle toy, chewing gum or moving your toes in your shoes to boost your concentration and focus whilst reading.

A picture (or a doodle) paints a thousand words

We tend to conceptualise reading and writing as separate tasks, but sometimes combining the reading we are doing *with* writing can boost our ability to think and learn. As an example, simply reading words is sometimes not enough to help us process complex or new ideas or material. The act of writing, scribbling or doodling can actually help us process *whilst* reading. In a similar way, if we are trying to process particularly complex ideas, actively drawing or producing infographics and diagrams whilst reading can help to bring these ideas to life in a way that we can not only assimilate, but can fully comprehend and retain for future use.

Depth versus breadth reading: All words are not created equal

If you have a particularly long reading list to work your way through, it can be really useful to think about the distinction between depth and breadth reading. This Welldoing strategy supports us to develop realistic and sustainable goals. When *reading to learn*, we sometimes put additional pressure on ourselves in terms of our expectations of what 'good' reading looks like. It can be tempting to devote our time and attention to all the texts that have been suggested on a reading list, but it's important to be realistic. What can we realistically achieve when we account for our cognitive capacity to take on board new information as well as the time we have available to us?

When teachers say work your way through an *entire* reading list of texts, this does not mean that we have to process, assimilate and remember every word, sentence and paragraph we have read for each text. This would simply not be possible! Instead, we need to remind ourselves that it is our ability to engage with and respond to what we are reading – the *thinking* that we carry out in response to what we have read – that is the most important aspect when reading to learn.

Not all words are created equal and so we need to practise the skill of prioritising certain sentences, paragraphs or sections of a text over others. Therefore, if you find reading particularly challenging, or find that you are simply pressed for time, then the following section will help you to become a speedier reader and teach you how to effectively skim and scan texts to find what you're looking for. This can reduce cognitive overload from overreading. This approach to reading will help you to ensure that you cover a range of texts (ensuring that you have read across the **Breadth** of texts) but equally will enable you to engage with what we call **Depth reading** where you **zoom** into a text and employ your comprehension skills.

Zoom reading: Using reading levels

You may have heard people refer to *skimming* and *scanning* when reading. This means confidently skim reading a text whilst, at the same time, scanning for key phrases, words or ideas. People do this in order to increase their reading speed and boost their comprehension skills. Like many study strategies, mastering the art of skimming and scanning texts effectively can take time, energy and, most importantly, confidence. We prefer to think of skimming and scanning as **Zoom reading**. Zoom reading assumes that, as we mentioned previously, not all words are created equal and therefore we need to learn *when* and *where on the page* to devote our time and energy to scrutinising the text. It involves shifting our focus and concentration and moving from one reading level to another.

If you find yourself devoting the same level of energy and time to every single word in a book, remind yourself that whilst it is possible to work in this way for short periods, it is actually an exhausting way to read and you will potentially very quickly run out of steam and could become demotivated as you make little progress with reading. Rather than thinking about the reading materials in front of you as a never-ending stream of words, try adopting the reading levels strategy to break this down into a number of separate reading levels (see **Figure 5.3**):

1. Book level
2. Chapter or section level
3. Paragraph level
4. Sentence level or word level

Purposefully and gradually zooming in on a text using these levels as a guide is a really powerful way of deconstructing, examining and being critical of the material you are reading. At each level, if you do not find something that seems of use to you, then move on to another text.

- *Book level*
- *Chapter or section level*
- *Paragraph level*
- *Sentence level or word level*

Figure 5.3   Zoom reading levels

CAPTION: Different reading levels to consider.

Bear in mind

It can take time and lots of practise to build this as one of your go-to Welldoing strategies. Develop your confidence slowly by practising on texts that you find less difficult to engage with, slowly ramping up the difficulty of the texts you use over time. Stick with it!

1. Book-level reading

This level will help to ensure that we do not spend too much time engaging with a text that then turns out to not be of use to us. The phrase 'don't judge a book by its cover' suggests we should not dismiss something without giving it time. Yet there are times, particularly if you have a long list of potential resources to get through, when judging the cover (and a few other key features of the book too!) can save you time, energy and stress. The key is to learn how to look for clues which will enable you to quickly identify whether the book is of use to you:

- Think about the key words used in the book title.
- Read the blurb on the back of the book or the abstract for journal articles.

- Look at the list of contents.
- Focus on the glossary and the index terms.

Note that this level of Zoom reading is useful when combined with the **Shopping list strategy to reading** in **Chapter 6**, so that when we are considering which texts or resources we should zoom into further we can clearly keep in mind the information or knowledge we are looking for.

2. Chapter- or section-level reading

Once you have identified at book level that a specific book is potentially useful to you, you can then zoom in to **Chapter- or section-level reading**. Consider which chapters are most likely to be relevant and useful to you by scanning the contents list for key words used in the chapter titles. This same approach can be used for sections of the book within chapters.

3. Paragraph-level reading

Once you have identified a specific chapter or certain sections of the book that are potentially useful, you can now zoom into the next reading level. Paragraphs form the basic building blocks of most forms of written communication. Understanding how paragraphs are generally structured (see **PIES: Recipe for a tasty paragraph** in **Chapter 6** for more on this) not only helps us to master the art of producing and writing our own paragraphs, but also enables us to fine-tune our reading skills:

- Each paragraph will generally contain one key point, known as the topic sentence. It is often, but not always, the first sentence in a paragraph. Therefore, sometimes it is possible to zoom into the beginning of each paragraph to get a sense of what is likely to be covered in the paragraph as a whole.
- We can also zoom in to specific transition key words and phrases which can be used as signposts to indicate where the text is heading. For example, if you zoom in and see the word 'furthermore' you know the author is likely to continue developing and extending the point that has just been made. If you zoom in and find the key words 'in contrast', you know that the author is likely making a contrary point. This can help speed up our reading, saving our energies and concentration for focused or depth reading at sentence or even word level as required.

4. Sentence- and word-level reading

Now we can zoom in further, focusing on reading at **Sentence and word level**. This is where we start to employ those all-important comprehension skills and start to practise **Depth reading** or focused analysis and evaluation of the sentences that we are reading. It is generally when reading at sentence level that we start being able to identify particular points that we can make a note of, paraphrase or use as quotes if required.

Word-level reading can be used at the same time as **Sentence-level reading**. This might include challenging the use of individual words or phrases in a report or perhaps exploring what a particular word or phrase means. To help you to do this, you may find it useful to refer to **Unpicking the recipe of assignment briefs and examination questions** in **Chapter 6**.

Bear in mind

Remember that **Zoom reading** may actually cause us to stop engaging with a book that we initially thought might be quite useful. This is OK. The purpose of this strategy is to boost our competence and confidence at moving between different texts or resources and learning when to stop zooming in and step away in order to move on to another resource that might be more beneficial to us.

Student voices

 In my course, there's a lot of reading and often I am not able to understand the text. I have integrated the **Zoom reading strategy** into my daily routine for less fatigue and more effective reading and learning.

Harshita, BA Psychology, India

The authors' approach to Welldoing

Writing a book represents the ultimate example of fear of the blank page! We really had to use the strategies in this book to help us write the book in this regard. We have all embraced really flexible ways of planning and writing by breaking up the page in front of us and making it feel like a less frightening blank space. We have repeatedly used tables, images, lots of colour coding, sticky notes and the all-important **Dot dot dot** strategy to help us overcome our writer's block! When editing and proofreading the book, we have used the ever-reliable **Break it down** strategy to make the job more manageable.

My blank canvas

Use this space to make a note of strategies you think could be useful to help you overcome reader's and writer's block and make reading and writing manageable. Remember to **Pick and mix**, **Develop your combo** and **Turn up (or down) the dial**, so that you can personalise an approach that works for you.

Don't forget that you may find some of your favourite strategies from this chapter help you to apply **Welldoing4home** and **Welldoing4work**. Similarly, can any of the strategies you have selected be applied at a **Micro and macro** level? Could the strategies in this chapter be used to help you to save **Spoons**, and can you combine any of the strategies with our **Common sensory** approach?

Remember that you can also make a note of strategies from other chapters in this space – think outside the box and consider how other strategies from elsewhere in the book might also help you to improve the efficiency with which you overcome any reader's and writer's block.

Key take aways

- Reconsider your relationship with the blank page and use strategies such as **Divide and conquer**, **Write as you speak**, **Dot dot dot**, and **Make the page mucky** to overcome the fear you might have of getting started with your writing.

- When you're planning your writing, try using the **Thinking spaces** strategies to help you to think more creatively about your thinking and planning, for example, **Thinking inside the box**, **Washing line**, and **Erase and rewind**.

- You can try to improve your note-taking approach by looking at the Welldoing **Taking note of how we take notes** strategies, which will help you to identify whether **Spaced notes**, **Pictorial notes** or **Audio notes**, amongst others, might work for you.

- There are a range of Welldoing strategies focused on overcoming reader's block and fear of the written page, helping you to develop confidence and efficiency when tackling tasks that rely on a large volume of reading, such as the **Common sensory approaches to reading**, **Dabbling** and **Zoom reading**.

Further resources

- In order to make the most of the **Overcoming reader's and writer's block** strategies, see the following templates in **Chapter 10**:

  - Template 11: Fear of the blank page
  - Template 12: Thinking spaces – The mind map
  - Template 13: Thinking spaces – Thinking inside the box
  - Template 14: Note-taking

- This resource provided by The Learning Centre at the University of North Carolina at Chapel Hill provides a comprehensive overview of the importance of effective note-taking: Effective Note-Taking in Class – https://learningcenter.unc.edu/tips-and-tools/effective-note-taking-in-class

- This article gives tips on how to read scientific papers, but many of the principles can be applied to other types of reading too: www.ncbi.nlm.nih.gov/pmc/articles/PMC3687192

- This resource provided by The Learning Centre at the University of North Carolina at Chapel Hill provides helpful tips to support reading comprehension: Reading Comprehension Tips – https://learningcenter.unc.edu/tips-and-tools/reading-comprehension-tips

- This website provides a range of practical strategies and tips for getting started with tasks: www.deprocrastination.co/blog

Recipes for planning and writing

Handy recipes to help you successfully cook up great pieces of writing

Is this chapter for me?

- Do you find it tricky to work out exactly *what* you need to do in an assignment and then *how* to go about doing it?

- Do you get overwhelmed with ideas and don't know how to bring these ideas together effectively to generate your work?

- Do you struggle to work out all the different aspects needed to create a successful piece of work, such as planning, writing, proofreading and how best to juggle these?

Recipes for planning and writing: The big picture

The journey from planning and getting started with a piece of work to handing it in on deadline day can be long, arduous and fraught with false starts and setbacks. It can often feel like we are the only one who has struggled to work on our assignment, whilst others seem to have produced a great piece of work as if by magic! In reality, many students struggle with this aspect of learning; it can feel like being thrown into the kitchen with a bunch of ingredients but no recipe or any idea what the finished product should look or taste like. It is quite common for learners to feel their finished piece of work doesn't quite capture what they were trying to say, or fully answer the question – like they were aiming for a patisserie-style gateau but instead ended up producing a pancake! However, it can be really difficult to pinpoint exactly what you could have done to make it top-rated; you might feel that your writing style needs developing or your ideas are half-baked, or worry that you are missing key ingredients.

In this chapter, we will share our tried-and-tested recipes for success to help you:

- Unpick your assignment briefs and translate this into a language that you understand (**Unpicking the recipe of assignment briefs and examination questions**).
- Use our reading shopping basket, less-is-more approach, for gathering and finding useful resources (**Ingredients, shopping baskets and shopping lists**).
- Break down the planning and writing process in a way that is bitesize and step by step (**Making planning and writing a piece of CAKE**).
- Produce great paragraphs with ease (**As easy as pie(s)!**).
- Store new ideas that you might think of when writing, safe in the knowledge that they are on ice, ready for when you might need them (**The ideas freezer**).
- Develop and edit your writing and check for any errors that might bring down your mark (**The icing on the cake**).

Don't forget to think about how you can apply all of the different tools you have available to you from the **Welldoing toolkit** when you are considering the strategies in this chapter.

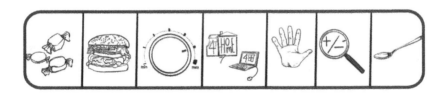

Unpicking the recipe of assignment briefs and examination questions

The time has come when a dreaded assessment is looming on the horizon. Even though you may have enjoyed a topic, or feel you know your subject well, you may still feel a growing sense of trepidation regarding whether you will get a 'good question' in the exam or be able to successfully unpack the assignment brief to work out what the examiner is looking for. Indeed, successfully unpicking and interpreting an assignment brief can feel like it is part of the assessment criteria itself! Being able to unpick and then respond effectively to the question is something we can all practise and get better at over time. In this section, we will give you the recipes to unpick your assignment or examination questions and translate this into language that you understand.

One of the most common challenges with interpreting assignment and exam questions is making sure we have clearly understood what the examiner or marker wants us to do with the knowledge we have. On some occasions, we may be asked to simply recall our knowledge to answer a straightforward question; this is sometimes the case with a multiple-choice style question. But more often than not, the assessment is asking us to *do* something with the knowledge that we have.

Key words in the question will indicate whether we are expected to describe, compare, contrast, evaluate or analyse. Therefore, the first thing to think about when unpicking the question is to note what the focus is in terms of topic, as well as identify which command words are included. This will help to ensure that we draw on the right knowledge (the topic in question), but also explore this knowledge in a way that directly answers the question and marking criteria.

Let's take the simple analogy of following a recipe. Imagine you have been asked to make some fried potatoes. It can be easy to focus first and foremost on the fact that you are going to make a potato dish – in other words, the key ingredient stands out and seems like the most important feature. But in order to do the recipe justice and produce the best dish possible, you also need to pay attention to *what* you need to do with the potato. As an example, you could produce the best roast potatoes in the world, and, although you have made something where the key ingredients are essentially right, you have not fulfilled the recipe, followed an appropriate method and made the required dish; in other words, it doesn't matter how tasty the roast potatoes are if you were asked to produce fried potatoes! When we apply the same logic to assessments or exams, students can frequently be marked down on the fact that although they have a good subject knowledge, they have not responded to the question in the way that the examiner or assessment required.

When faced with a question that is not immediately straightforward or easy to unpick, try the following recipe to crack the code and identify exactly what you need to do. Use our **Cracking the recipe of assignment briefs and examination questions** template in **Chapter 10** to help you get started (**Template 15**).

Recipe for unpicking an assignment brief

1. **Pick out the command words.** Are you being asked to 'critically analyse', 'evaluate', 'contrast'...? You might find it helpful to highlight, underline or circle these terms to help pay attention to what you're being asked to do. Don't worry if you are not quite clear at this point in terms of what these command words mean – we have a recipe for that and will cover this all-important step shortly!
2. **Identify the topic.** Consider what content and concepts the question relates to. Do you feel you have a good grasp of this content or might you need to revisit some of the material or do some additional reading (if possible)?
3. **Additional sources of information.** Does the question indicate whether there are any other additional sources of information or data you need to include or make reference to in your assignment? This might include a key reading, some data, statistics, practical work...
4. **The taste-test.** We think of this final stage of our recipe as a 'taste-test'. It is a useful way of reviewing what you have planned and written for the assignment and can help you to make sure that you have included all the key ingredients listed above in order to answer the question. Whilst creating your assignment or answering the question you have been set, keep checking what you are writing so that you get the mix right; the combination of responding to the command words *and* drawing on the most appropriate content and resources will lead you towards success.

Roasted, boiled or fried: How to distinguish between description, analysis and evaluation – the big three!

Now you have deconstructed the question and identified the key components or ingredients which are required to answer it, it is important to check that you fully understand *what* you are being asked to do. Just as it is important to know what the difference is between roasting, boiling or frying potatoes, you also need to be able to distinguish between description, analysis and evaluation. In other words, even if you have great subject knowledge, if you have used too much description and not enough analysis or have compared without contrasting, you risk not answering the question properly.

Being clear on what each command term means and what it can look like in relation to our subject is key to success. Yet many of us use common command terms interchangeably and, whilst we might have a rough sense of what evaluation looks like compared to description, it is not always explicitly clear and can seem abstract and unfamiliar. We will now explore how we can make sense of these different command terms and ensure we are applying them in the right way. We'll also highlight how these are skills we use on a daily basis and can be practised through a range of everyday contexts that feel more concrete and familiar.

In the following section, we have focused on some of the most challenging and often misunderstood command words which we frequently find popping up in assignment or exam questions. In reality, there are many more command words and the nature of these will vary depending on the course you are studying and the level you are studying at. The key is to make sure that you spend time identifying, interpreting and getting used to the command words so that they don't catch you out. That way, no matter what the question or task, you will be able to work out your own effective recipe for answering and responding to the question effectively.

Bear in mind

It is also worth remembering that our teachers are only human and language can be fluid and certain command words may be used differently depending on your subject discipline. If in doubt, try and find this clarification in the marking criteria or ask your teacher.

Basic recipe for a spoonful of description

One of the most straightforward ways of interpreting what we mean when we are asked to describe is to paint a picture in words to say what you see. To practise this skill, it can be useful to literally apply this to a painting, an image or a paused moment in a video. Description requires us to draw on our senses, to paint this picture. For example, in an everyday context, you might describe what you did yesterday; this might include describing who you saw, what you did, where you were and how long this took. But that is where description ends; if you then venture to express an opinion or evaluate something, you are moving away from description towards explanation, evaluation or analysis.

On the face of it, description seems quite straightforward. We do it every day without even thinking about it. However, one of the most common mistakes people make when being asked to describe is in ensuring they do this in a way that is succinct. Take a look at the **PIES: Recipe for a tasty paragraph** later in this chapter. The point we make to start our paragraph can be considered as description. Therefore, as a general rule, some description is needed. Indeed, you can't analyse or evaluate something if you haven't first succinctly described it in simple and clear terms!

The key with getting description right is to think about the level of detail you want to go into. If you find that 90% of the assignment you have produced is description based, then you probably haven't included the right mix of skills. Therefore, it's important to remember that description is useful to set the scene and introduce a key point you are making. Remember, if you feel you want to get confident at this skill, you can be more mindful of when you are using description in an everyday context. This will make it easier to practise in contexts which are more familiar and less abstract to you.

In summary, remember that a good rule of thumb is to stick to a **spoonful of description** to clearly articulate your point to your audience or marker. When studying, you will find that you are often required to combine a spoonful of description with other command words which moves us on to our other recipes.

The key is to then think about what you have been asked to *do in response to* what you are describing. Are you meant to provide an explanation, some evaluation or some personal reflection?

Recipes for a good dollop of analysis and evaluation

If you feel overwhelmed when you see the words critical thinking, analysis or evaluation and are not quite sure what you are being asked to do, then please don't worry – you are not alone! These terms are often used interchangeably, which can make them feel quite confusing and harder to work out what is actually required of you. In reality, these terms or skills are often connected and overlap, but breaking them down into more manageable and distinct skills can help us to better understand what we are being asked to do in the context of the subject we are studying or the assignment we are working on.

Analysis

The word analysis can cause a great deal of confusion for many students, and we may find ourselves attempting to 'analyse' what the word itself means in the context of the subject we are studying! A useful way of thinking about analysis is to think of it like digging deeper to uncover layers of meaning. Analysis is an incredibly powerful tool to have as a student and is a skill we can use throughout life, whether studying or working, to develop our capacity to see something from multiple angles or consider different interpretations.

Analysis can be applied to everything from everyday dialogue to a political speech. Remember, we are interested in digging deeper and thinking about what something might mean; meaning is constructed and can change over time and in different cultural contexts. Analysis therefore helps us to scratch the surface and go beyond taking something at face value.

Bear in mind

Some of you may have very heightened skills of analysis and often find yourself naturally in a position where you feel you are over-thinking or analysing; the term 'analysis paralysis' rather ironically describes a state of being where we identify too many angles and perspectives and this can lead to inaction. Whether analysis is something you feel you don't do naturally or is something you feel you do to the degree that it paralyses you, the key is to practise applying this skill in a way that works for you.

Recipe for the over-thinker or analyser

You might feel you don't need to develop this skill as you are always questioning and critiquing, but you might like to find ways of controlling how you apply this analytical thinking. Using strategies which help you to restrain this might sound counter-intuitive but this will give you greater control of the analysis and how you are applying it to your subject. For example, you might find our **Basic recipe for sources** (later in this chapter) helps you to focus and limit your reading or the **Thinking inside the box** strategy (in **Chapter 5**) helps you break down and control your thinking when planning your assignments.

Recipe for the under-analyser

Developing your analysis linked to a new, tricky or challenging subject or topic can make analysis feel like an uphill struggle. A good starting point might be to therefore practise these skills in an everyday context that is more familiar and less overwhelming. For example, you might find it useful to apply your analysis to a painting, a film, an advert or some song lyrics. The key is to ask yourself to go beyond what you immediately observe at face value. For example, if viewing a painting, you might like to consider what the individual elements of the painting might symbolise or mean. Or if watching an advert, you might find it helpful to question the strategies the advert is using and how this is being used to persuade the audience. You might also find it helpful to practise your analysis when watching dialogue on television. Notice how characters sometimes say one thing, but perhaps mean another. Once you start analysing, you might find you can't stop!

'Fishing' for your supper: Our technique for focused analysis

One way of harnessing your analysis skills and applying this to your assignment is to combine this with our **Zoom reading** strategy in **Chapter 5**. When carrying out Zoom reading, we encourage you to 'zoom in' to a specific paragraph, sentence or word to focus your reading skills and hone your analysis. We call this our **Fishing technique**. Zoom in and 'hook out' a particular word, phrase or sentence that you can use to analyse. This can be particularly useful if you are critically analysing a report, reading or policy, or if you are 'zooming in' on a technique which an author has used.

Recipe for signposting our analysis

Phrases such as 'this demonstrates', 'this indicates' or 'this would suggest' can help us to build analytical thinking into our work and signpost it clearly. Again, once you feel more comfortable and confident, practise how you build this analytical thinking into your writing. Refer to our **PIES: Recipe for a tasty paragraph** later in this chapter to develop this skill and ensure you do this in every paragraph, weaving this throughout an assignment.

Recipe to help evaluate: Asking *What, Where, Who, When, Why* and *How?*

Evaluation essentially involves weighing up the *value* of something and making an informed judgement on this. This might include identifying the pros and cons for something, such as a theory, argument or point of view. Therefore, if analysis is about recognising that there may be multiple ways of considering or viewing something in terms of meaning, then evaluation involves considering the extent to which this view or perspective is valid, effective, useful or true (University of Portsmouth, 2022).

In an age where we are overwhelmed by information, it is becoming increasingly important to consider the validity and reliability of what we read or hear. When evaluating, try this recipe to help you go beyond a focus on just what someone is saying:

1. **What**? What is being said? Is it fact, opinion?
2. **Where**? Where is the author located? Where was the work published?
3. **Who**? Who is saying this? Could this influence what they are saying?
4. **When**? When was it said – is the source very old or cutting edge?

5. **Why**? Why are they saying this? Could there be any bias?
6. **How**? How are they communicating? Is it colloquial, academic? How does this impact how you view the information?

When applying this in an assignment, it is usually best to weave your evaluation throughout your work in each paragraph. Returning to our analogy of roasting or frying your potatoes, you would want to ensure that this is done evenly across the potatoes rather than just to one or two of the potatoes!

Bear in mind

You don't need to include *every* aspect of what, where, who, when, why and how in each paragraph – this could become a bit repetitive and formulaic. Instead, when viewing a source or drawing on some information, get into the habit of practising this skill so that you build your confidence in knowing that you have made an informed judgement and been thorough in your evaluation.
As mentioned before, practise this in everyday contexts to build up your confidence over time. You could do this when watching the news or adverts.

Adding further flavour to your analysis and evaluation

Cooking up critical thinking

Critical thinking goes beyond description and explanation. This can at first make it seem more challenging, but by thinking about the different elements that make up critical thinking, we can be more confident that we are applying these tools in the right way. As a starting point, it can be helpful to break down critical thinking into two overlapping and complementary, but ultimately separate, skills. To think critically, we often draw on both analysis and evaluation (see **Figure 6.1**). Depending on the subject you are studying, or the type of assignment you are working on, you may find that different amounts of the two are applied. This is something you will get used to over time as your confidence grows.

A sprinkling of synthesis

When you are asked to synthesise, you are being asked to do something that *overlaps with* evaluation and analysis to form critical thinking at a more advanced level. This is

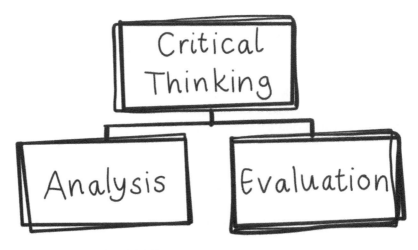

Figure 6.1   Breaking down critical thinking

CAPTION: Critical thinking draws on both analysis and evaluation.

a really advanced level skill, so do not worry if this does not immediately seem like the easiest thing to master. Synthesising can be done at a macro level, for example generating a new concept or an original idea. This is something that often features as a key element of Master's and PhD-level study. But more often than not, we can synthesise at a micro level and are not expected to come up with amazing, original ideas to showcase in our work. Once again, this is something we do in our daily lives without even thinking about it or realising it. Imagine, for example, you chose a recipe and then decide to make some small changes to that recipe to improve it and give it your own stamp, such as adding an additional ingredient or presenting the dish in a new way.

When we are learning, we can become more aware of when we are using analysis and evaluation to start synthesising. You might compare (see next strategy) two opposing theories or views and subsequently synthesise an alternative way of thinking, which combines or sits between current thinking. One way you could apply micro-level synthesis is by using the **Fishing technique** to **Zoom** in and analyse a key word or phrase, and then suggest a particular way of viewing what is being said.

Sweet or savoury: Compare or contrast

Compare and contrast are both things that you may be asked to do in an assignment. In very simple terms, contrast is specifically concerned with identifying differences between two different things. Compare overlaps with contrast; when comparing you are likely to identify differences, but this will be in addition to identifying similarities. Because the terms overlap in this way, you may find that they are sometimes used interchangeably. Therefore, comparing and contrasting can be considered as a type of analytical and evaluative approach. Carefully check which you are being asked to do. Again, if you are being specifically asked to compare and contrast, remember to weave this aspect of the question throughout your answer, so that you make comparisons in every paragraph. (See **PIES: Recipe for a tasty paragraph** later in this chapter.)

Refining your reflection

Similarly to analysis, the words reflect or reflective practice can instil fear into the hearts of many students. Reflection often brings to mind lots of potentially complex models, theories or tools that we need to draw upon. Yet, in reality, reflection is something we all engage in on a daily basis. When we engage in any activity in our daily lives, we often naturally pause (either when carrying out or after completing the action) and think about what we have just done and maybe how we did this or how well this worked (Schon, 1991). Reflection therefore helps us to adapt our behaviour over time, change our course of action and actively consider the reasons why we are making such a change (Kolb, 1984). If we are learning a new skill, reflection helps us to refine and hone this skill; indeed, you will be reflecting on the Welldoing strategies outlined in this book as you apply them and then adapt and refine them over time to work for you.

Reflection can be carried out at both a macro and micro level – you might decide to change something significant in your life due to reflecting on it, such as changing your job. But it can also be applied at a micro level where you make a small but impactful shift in how you do something. For example, you might decide to implement a big change in terms of how you work, such as altering the environment or changing where you work, or you might have made a much smaller change in terms of tweaking how you approach something. What is important is that you have reflected, whether the change is big or small.

In a sense, you are using your critical analysis skills to help you to think reflectively. But reflective thinking takes this analysis or evaluating slightly further by then identifying what you might do slightly differently as a consequence. It is also worth noting that we often think of reflection as a decision we make to do something differently. In reality, reflection can also involve identifying things that have gone well and we might continue to do.

So when reflecting, you might start with a spoon of description, add a dollop of analysis or evaluation and then show how this has led you to either do something differently or help you to review and consolidate what you are already doing.

Look at **PIES: Recipe for a tasty paragraph** and remember to sprinkle reflection liberally throughout your assignment rather than just in one section or paragraph such as the conclusion.

Pause for thought

Take any everyday activity you have carried out in the last week – remember, it can be easier to practise and master a skill when you do this consciously linked to an area of your life that is familiar. For example, you may have cooked something, either using a recipe or making it up as you go along. Think about how well it worked and whether you might adapt the methods, tools or ingredients you used next time around and why.

Ingredients, shopping baskets and shopping lists: How sometimes less is more!

Reading shopping baskets versus shopping trolleys

When we are faced with the task of finding ideas, information or evidence to develop an assignment, it can be really tempting to go for what we call a shopping trolley approach – most often we instead need a shopping *basket* approach. Let us explain.

Shopping basket

When we sit down with a number of books, articles or online resources, or are faced with an extensive reading list, we can enter into a frenzied panic-reading (similar to panic buying!) mode where we think that we must capture as many ideas, quotes or notes as possible. This is very similar to going into a supermarket with a very large trolley and seeing lots of interesting, possibly useful, tasty ingredients that we seize with both hands and put in our trolley, thinking that they could come in handy but not yet knowing what we will use them for. The **Shopping basket** strategy for reading and planning encourages us to be more selective in our reading choices in terms of the quality, usefulness and relevance of the ideas we come across when reading, rather than simply filling our trolley for the sake of capturing as much information as possible, just in case. If we take the analogy a step further and imagine that the ideas in books or articles are ingredients, it is really helpful to remember that it is not a case of simply selecting as many ingredients as possible when we are cooking, but actually that it is what you *do* with the ingredients that is really important. When we are writing or producing an assignment, it is our ability to engage with the ideas or ingredients that we have selected and make something really special out of them that will help us to succeed: having fewer ingredients but paying much more attention to *what* we select and *how* we will use them will not only make our assignments better but will also make the workload of reading more manageable, reducing pressure and ensuring that you are actually showcasing your best reading, thinking and writing skills.

Bear in mind

The **Shopping basket** strategy can take confidence to apply and it is a skill that you will need to practise over time – don't expect to master it overnight. Slowly push yourself to move from filling a trolley with ideas to filling a *basket* with ideas that you have more carefully selected. See our **Reading shopping baskets** template in **Chapter 10 (Template 16)**.

Shopping lists

We can also effectively combine the **Shopping basket** strategy with the **Shopping list** strategy. Think about writing a shopping list of the exact things you need to cook *one* specific dish or recipe and then popping into a shop to pick up the ingredients on the list. Even though you know you should focus on getting the specific ingredients for the recipe, it can be very tempting whilst in the shop to add other items to your shopping basket – things that might look tasty or things that might be useful to have in your store cupboard, that you could use another time or when creating another dish.

If this scenario is familiar to you (we can certainly relate to this!), then using the analogy of a shopping list can provide a useful reminder to help us stay focused and on task and ensure that we are gathering the most useful ideas or ingredients to build our best possible response to an assignment based on the question we have actually been asked. After all, if you need to produce a chocolate chip cookie and get side-tracked by some incredibly tasty fruits and vegetables, not only are they not going to work for the dish you are producing, but they're also potentially going to make it taste dreadful and produce a completely different dish to that which you're supposed to be making! See our **Reading shopping lists** template in **Chapter 10 (Template 17)**.

Basic recipe for using sauces, sorry, *sources*

'How many references, sources, pieces of evidence, information or quotes do I need to refer to? Teachers will often reply that this is not an exact science: they can't give a specific answer, which can leave students feeling frustrated. Whilst there isn't an exact answer, we have frequently found that students tend to over-compensate and over-fill their assignment shopping basket to ensure they have enough material to work from and use in their assignment. If you find you tend to over-read and try to cram too many references into your assignments, you can use the simple recipe formula below to help you to roughly estimate or calculate how many sources to use. This approach helps to remind us that we don't need hundreds of ideas/quotes or pieces of evidence from our readings; a shopping *basket* rather than *trolley* full of good ingredients will help to make the most of the evidence we are using.

A good starting point is to look at the length of the assignment that you are producing. Whilst this isn't an exact science (unlike baking!), our basic recipe can help to provide you with an *estimate* so that you don't fall into the trap of under- or over-filling your assignment shopping basket:

- Take a 2000-word assignment.
- Roughly divide the total word count by the number of paragraphs this is likely to include (as a rough guide, 200–300 words would be a good estimate for the average paragraph length). Working towards a rough average paragraph length of 200 words, then we have a rough estimate that we will include around ten paragraphs in the piece of work.
- Using **The secret ingredients of paragraphs** recipe (later in this chapter), you would therefore make around ten succinct and specific points, one per paragraph.
- You're likely to need a range of one to two sources of information/evidence to support each of those paragraph points. Therefore, this roughly equates to between 10 and 20 sources/pieces of evidence to support the points you plan to make.

Bear in mind

Remember, this is not an exact science and there may be a variation depending on the subject, the assessment criteria and the purpose of the writing, and even your own writing style.

Making, planning and writing a piece of CAKE

It is not uncommon for many of us to feel that, in spite of the fact that we have lots of good ideas, we don't always quite manage to articulate exactly what we were trying to say when capturing these on the page; we may find that we have greater control when talking through our ideas than when attempting to cement them in writing. We might find that we struggle with information overload or analysis paralysis and that there are simply too many things for us to keep in our mind and relay to the reader in a way that makes sense (Sweller, 1988).

Before we start exploring strategies that will help you with the planning and writing process, try to imagine a scenario where you have decided to bake a cake. When making a cake you would follow a recipe (unless you are a star baker and can do this without!) but you would also break down the stages involved. No baker would try to carry out all the steps involved in baking a cake simultaneously. See the **Lessons from baking** strategy below to see how we can borrow some lessons from baking and apply them to help us to develop and master our planning and writing skills.

Lessons from baking: Step by step

1. Once we have decided what we are going to bake, we need to gather our ingredients. We might check what we already have in our store cupboard, then pop to the shop to pick up the ingredients we need to buy.
2. We would then use the recipe to identify the quantities of each ingredient.
3. Next, the ingredients are mixed together, based on the instructions in the recipe.
4. Following on from this, the cake mix is baked so that all the ingredients fuse together to make one whole.
5. Finally, once the cake is fully assembled, cooked and cooled, it is decorated to make it look as good as possible, adding our artistic flourishes.

Now, think about the approach to making a cake but instead picture yourself attempting to plan and write an assignment...

Sometimes we place a lot of pressure on ourselves by *simultaneously* carrying out multiple tasks and we don't think to separate out these stages. It is not uncommon for us to try and capture our ideas in writing whilst also trying to identify relevant evidence *and* trying to sequence our ideas coherently as well as trying to make the sentences look and sound good by editing and proofreading as we go. Sound familiar...?

Some people find that they are able to manage planning, writing, sequencing and polishing simultaneously. However, this adds a lot of cognitive load (Sweller, 1988) to the brain and can undermine the quality of the work we produce. Imagine if we made a cake using this same approach, carrying out each stage in the process simultaneously – we would be left with a cake that was likely to be inedible! Therefore, in order to **Make planning and writing a piece of CAKE**, we can use the following recipe to break the task down, separating out the different stages involved in the planning and writing process to give ourselves the best chance of success. **CAKE** stands for Capture, Arrange, Key words and phrases, and Edit.

> **Capture:** The first stage is to **Capture** your ideas. This is where we free ourselves up to stop worrying about ordering, editing or proofreading our ideas. It's not that these aspects of writing are not important – they are just not vital to focus on right at the start of the process. Focus solely on the points you want to make and the evidence you have, simply concentrating on capturing these great ideas on the page before you lose them.
>
> It is worth noting that sometimes we may have a clear idea of the points we want to make, but you may also find you are not sure where to start, particularly if you are tackling a new or complex subject for the first time.
>
> When we Capture our ideas, we have the option to start with what we know we would like to say or to look at a range of other sources to kick start our thinking. Think of this in the same way as a kitchen larder; sometimes our larder is full of lots of tasty ingredients which gives us the option of cooking up something tasty. But sometimes our larder may feel empty and we might need to pop out to the shop to refill our larder cupboard before we can get started with our cooking.
>
> It is exactly the same for planning and writing an assignment; think about whether you have some clear ideas or 'ingredients' and wish to get started with these, or whether you might need to 'top-up' your raw ideas or ingredients by reading around the subject. Remember that ultimately we want to build tasty paragraphs which contain the right ingredients. When we are in the capturing phase of planning, we are ultimately aiming to generate some clear points and also to support this with relevant information (in the form or some data, statistics, evidence or quotes from other sources) so that each paragraph contains the right mix of ingredients (see **PIES: Recipe for a tasty paragraph** later in this chapter, and also **Reading shopping baskets** in **Chapter 5**, for help on this).
>
> **Arrange:** Once we have captured our ideas, we can then start **Arranging** these ideas and work out the best possible way to present or sequence them so that a reader can easily follow our thinking. This is often the hardest part of the planning and writing process; most of us find it easier to generate ideas or content but struggle with the structuring and sequencing of these ideas. If we focus in on this task separately via the **CAKE** strategy, we can really concentrate our energies on ensuring that we organise our ideas in a logical order. Take time for this step and the following stages of planning

and writing are likely to run much more smoothly. Have a look at our **Thinking spaces** strategy in **Chapter 5** for further guidance on this. How we use and control the page will shape our ability to effectively arrange and sequence our writing.

Key words and phrases: Once you have captured your ideas and evidence and arranged these in the best possible order, you can then start to think about the **Key words and phrases** needed to join not only your sentences together, but also your paragraphs. These key words act as signposts and will help move your reader or audience forwards from one idea to the next. For example, if you use the phrase 'in contrast', this clearly indicates that you are moving on to make a point which is different to the one you have just made. In contrast(!), if you use a word such as 'similarly', the reader immediately knows that you are making a point which is *similar* to the one you have just made. Therefore, when refining and developing your writing, think about how you can help the reader to smoothly move from one idea to another. For a useful bank of common command words, have a look at Cambridge's essay signposting resource listed in the **Further resources** section at the end of this chapter.

Edit: Finally, now that we have captured our ideas, and arranged them to ensure that we have effective key words and transitions in order to convey a clear narrative, we can focus our energies on **editing** our work. This is equivalent to decorating a cake after the main stages of mixing and baking have been finished, and is how we make sure that our work looks as good as possible. Make sure that you save enough time and energy for this really important stage; after all, even the best ideas in the world can be let down if the polish or decorating has not been carried out. For this stage of the **CAKE** strategy, don't forget you can use the **Icing on the cake** strategies (later in this chapter) to support you in getting to grips with how to make your writing shine. There may also be key words that your discipline requires you to use – you can check your ideas and writing so far and see if you have included these.

Bear in mind

The **CAKE** strategy can also be used beyond traditional pieces of writing such as essays – consider applying it when you next have to do a presentation or produce a portfolio or lab report.

Student voices

'The **CAKE** formula for writing essays has not only been incredibly insightful in improving my writing for my exam structure, but it has helped me in my applications to university. Before finding out how to better my structure I was really struggling to accurately articulate my wants and desires; **CAKE** helped me to do this.'

Elizabeth, A levels, UK

As easy as pie(s)!:

The secret ingredients of paragraphs

One of the most effective ways of taking greater control of the writing process is to master the art of building paragraphs. Before we share strategies that will help you to deconstruct your paragraphs, imagine a scene where a celebrity chef has just produced an incredible pie. Whilst most people in the audience would be able to appreciate what a great pie looks and tastes like, they might struggle to identify exactly *why* the pie was so good if they are not expert bakers themselves. Now imagine that instead of viewing a pie, you are being shown an exemplar essay. Whilst you might immediately be able to judge that this is a strong piece of work, you might find it much harder to unpick exactly *why*. To the untrained eye, it can be hard to pick out what individual ingredients have been used to make the piece of work so successful.

Now imagine a beautiful selection of freshly baked individual pies in a baker's window. Whilst the pies might contain different fillings and have different individual flavours, they all contain the same certain key ingredients, without which they couldn't exist! In the same way that each pie top contains the hidden ingredients of flour, salt, a fat such as butter and a liquid such as water, paragraphs also contain their own secret ingredients.

In this section, we help you to uncover the secret ingredients of paragraphs. Paragraphs provide the fundamental building blocks in how we communicate our ideas to our audience in writing; they provide the backbone of our writing and enable us to organise and control our ideas so that these are conveyed in a way that can be easily digested by our audience. If you can crack the skill of building paragraphs, then writing can become as easy as pie!

PIES: Recipe for a tasty paragraph

Simply replace the flour, fat, liquid and salt you would use to bake some **PIES** with the following ingredients: **Point, Information, Explanation, So what?**

1. **Point.** Start each paragraph with a key **Point** or idea you would like to make to answer the question. Note, you mind find it useful to check out our definition of description earlier on in this chapter to help you to keep the points you make succinct and to the point!
2. **Information.** Back up this point using **Information** to support what you are saying. This can take many different forms depending on the assignment brief and subject. This could include either a direct or paraphrased quote, some statistics to support your key point or numerical data you have collected in practical work as evidence. Have a look at our recipe on **Unpicking assignment briefs** earlier in this chapter to make sure you have successfully unpicked the assessment title and are including all the right ingredients to build your pies.
3. **Explanation.** Whilst the first two steps of PIES are vital to give your paragraph structure, providing an **Explanation** is the bit that really boosts the impact or effectiveness of your answer. This explanation takes the form of providing reasons for the point and information you have included. Your explanation might contain a good spoonful of analysis or a dollop of evaluation (or a combination of these!) depending on the question you are being asked. Remember to refer to our **recipes for analysis, evaluation** etc. earlier in this chapter to ensure you are providing an effective explanation which answers the question.
4. **So what?** To perfect your PIES, ask yourself, **So what?** when providing your explanation to help you refer back to the question you are answering. This will help to ensure you specifically answer the question and do not head off on a tangent.

Student voices

‘As someone who is currently writing large essays at university, the **PIES** strategy has become my number one ally. By using the So what? reminder of PIES, my responses are more formal and this helps me ensure I relate my answer back to the question in hand.

Alex, BA Politics with International Relations, UK ’

Our recipe for PIES will help you to create good all-round paragraphs. Whilst this may feel slightly unnatural and a bit artificial at the start (just as using any recipe to begin with), as you get used to it, you will start to naturally write in this way and find you don't need to follow or refer to the PIES recipe.

Bear in mind

The PIES recipe can be adapted depending on what you are producing. It can be used to write paragraphs in an essay or a report, but also works well when planning a presentation. As you become more confident in constructing paragraphs, you might start to play around with this basic recipe and develop it further to enhance your PIES.

Pause for thought

We tend to think of writing as a linear process with a beginning, middle and end, but there is another more powerful way of thinking about the overall structure of your assessment. Use our **Recipe for unpicking assignment briefs** in this chapter and *combine* this with the **PIES** recipe, so that when you plan and write your response, you make sure you are including a good sprinkling of analysis and evaluation (or whatever else the question asks you to do!) in each and every paragraph.

The ideas freezer

When we are engaged in the process of writing, we have all experienced that moment when we suddenly think of a new idea that we want to capture on the page right there and then before it evaporates into thin air. The problem is, if we try to do this whilst we're in the throes of writing, this can suddenly send our work off on a tangent and before we know it, our writing is at risk of losing its narrative flow as it heads off in a new direction. One possible answer is to simply ignore these ideas and put them out of our mind in order to keep to the immediate task in hand, but that's not how our brains work, and for some of us, one great idea often sparks another and so on. Therefore, the **ideas freezer** strategy helps by acknowledging this can happen and helping us to make the most of it.

The ideas freezer is just that – it is a space (e.g. a physical or digital page) which is completely separate from the writing we are producing. This space exists solely for the purpose of allowing us to capture or 'freeze' these additional ideas that pop into our heads when we are in the middle of writing or planning. In doing so, we avoid the risk of sending our work off on a tangent. Instead, we can move forward with the task of writing, knowing that the idea that popped into our heads is captured, 'on ice' and stored safely so we can come back to it at another point and think about where it might be best integrated into the piece of work we are producing.

Just as we have explored a range of planning strategies to help you use the space on a page effectively in a way that best suits you (see **Thinking Spaces** in **Chapter 5**), you can also use the same approach when designing your own ideas freezer: your freezer could be mapped out as a table or you might like to use Post-it notes or some kind of mind map. Alternatively, you may like to use software to do this. Be creative and think about the type of planning or thinking spaces that have helped you in other contexts. You might even like to create a visual ideas freezer with different shelves for different topics and different spaces just like the freezer in the home that you can then add ideas to as and when you need to. See our **Ideas freezer** template in **Chapter 10 (Template 18)**.

Bear in mind

Just because an idea is stored or 'on ice' please don't feel that all those ideas have to be used – you may find that some of your captured ideas can be thawed out and used at another time or for a different piece of writing; after all, too many brilliant ideas in one piece of work can sometimes lead to information overload for the reader as well as the writer! Indeed, we have used an ideas freezer ourselves for the writing of this book and there are still some ideas that we think are great but they are held on ice for the moment, ready to be used when we feel we need some inspiration or a new idea to write about or explore.

The icing on the cake (proofreading)

Most of us can find proofreading boring or frustrating, particularly if we have been working on a piece of writing for quite a while – it can feel like a step too far and we can sometimes be tempted to rush this process or even leave it out altogether. We often see proofreading as something negative, as a way of picking up on our mistakes, but in fact proofreading is a really powerful way of developing and refining your writing skills, ultimately helping to boost your grades. So, before you overlook the value of proofreading or whizz through this vital stage in order to get round to the all-important task of submitting your work, bear with us and explore our strategies for proofreading.

Imagine baking an incredible cake that tastes great, but the presentation of the cake means it doesn't look particularly appetising. Despite it being incredibly tasty, it is unlikely anyone is going to choose to eat it!

It is exactly the same with proofreading. Your work could be great, incorporating exciting and original ideas and demonstrating your ability to critically analyse an issue, but if it lacks polish (think of this as the decorated finish on a cake), then you reduce the chances of your writing having the impact it deserves. Proofreading is a universal skill that you can use to polish anything from writing an essay, a dissertation or report to producing a CV or letter of application for a job.

It is also useful to think of proofreading as having two separate functions:

1. To spot mistakes with grammar, spelling and formatting. This is the version of proof-reading we often think about first.
2. To focus on how you can polish and refine your writing – the communication/articulation of your ideas.

So far in this book, we have actively encouraged you to step away from polishing and perfecting your writing too soon. This is because worrying about the polish can sometimes be a distraction and lead to you losing your good ideas. That said, when you have captured, arranged and sequenced your key ideas (see **Making, planning and writing a piece of CAKE**), polishing can help to ensure that you have made it easier for your reader to take on board your ideas. Remember, the easier it is for a reader to process and make sense of your ideas, the better you will have demonstrated the skills of communication, which is likely to help you in achieving a higher mark, or getting noticed for a job.

Proof writing

The term proofreading is a little misleading as the purpose of the task is actually to develop our writing. So think of it as proof writing as well as proofreading. Sometimes thinking about the task in this way can help to remind us that to do this effectively, we need to write, scribble, cross out and embellish. This will help to make the task more active and impactful, rather than simply reading the text you have produced.

Proofreading with purpose

Another way of making the process of proofreading (and writing!) more active and engaging is to read your work with a specific focus in mind. We talked about having a **Shopping list** for reading earlier in the chapter – you might find it useful to have a shopping list for proofreading too. Not only will this remind you of the key things you might want to check your work for (such as punctuation, spelling, over-use of specific key words), but it will also help you to break down the task; trying to read your work through in one go whilst looking for multiple things you might need to edit can overload the brain and reduce your effectiveness at carrying this out. Therefore, try to split up the read-throughs you do and focus on one key thing at a time.

In the same way, it can be useful to proofread by drawing on the **Zoom reading levels** we explored in **Chapter 5**. For example, you may wish to do a quick paragraph-level proofread; scanning the document as a whole, do your paragraphs look roughly consistent in length? Additionally, could you use the **PIES** recipe to check that each of your paragraphs is fully developed and contains a concise point and evidence to support this? Have you linked back to your title and answered the question? In contrast, you might like to focus on individual sentences to check that you have not used too many long and overly complex sentences or that you have punctuated your sentences correctly. At word level, you might like to proofread to check you haven't overused a word or even a grammatical construct such as exclamation marks.

Patterns in errors

This strategy combines nicely with the previous strategy; proofreading is a skill which we can develop over time. To help you to do this as effectively as possible, it can be useful to start looking for patterns in your mistakes – for example, if you receive feedback from a teacher that tells you that you use too many long sentences or too many commas, then focus your proofreading on this aspect of your writing.

Pause for thought

Can you identify any patterns linked to things you have received feedback on from teachers in the past? Are there particular things you would like to tackle in your writing or areas you know you could improve on?

Content-related errors/improvements

You might find it useful to do a proofread linked to content. For example, are the facts you have used accurate? This is particularly important for explanatory and descriptive text where the purpose is to convey information. You might also find it useful to check that have you answered all parts of the question or task. Remember to use our **Recipe for unpicking assignment briefs** to help with this.

Seeing your writing through fresh eyes

One of the key challenges with proofreading is that we often read what we *think* we have written rather than what we have *actually* written. It is much easier to read someone else's work and spot errors or things that can be improved. When reading our own work, we are too close to it and it can feel too familiar. Sometimes if you have been cooking for a long period, you can't fully taste what you are making anymore!

The trick with effective proofreading is to trick our brain into thinking it is reading something new and unfamiliar – it is almost a case of making our brains think we are reading something for the first time. The following strategies will help to put some much-needed distance between you and your work by tricking your brain into thinking it is engaging with something unfamiliar.

Common sensory proofreading

We can actively draw on our senses to help us see our writing through fresh eyes. Strategies such as transferring your work from the screen to another format such as printing it out on the physical page can help to create that much-needed distance from your writing. Changing background colour or text size and style can also help.

Reading out loud

This can be a really useful strategy to help you feel more removed from your writing and trick the brain so that your writing sounds different. You could also record your writing and listen back to it or use text-to-speech software so you can hear your work rather than relying solely on your eyes to do all the work.

Give yourself some space!

Too many words on a page can feel like they are competing for our attention. It can be useful to give yourself some space so that you can just focus on one paragraph or sentence at a time. You can do this by covering up part of a page or hitting the return button to move text so that it is out of the way and out of sight.

Back to front reading

Odd as this strategy may seem, try reading your writing out of sequence to trick your brain and feel like you are reading something for the first time. This can be done by reading each paragraph out of order, or you can also try doing this with individual sentences. Obviously, this strategy doesn't work if you are trying to check on the overall flow and sequence of your ideas, but it can work particularly well if you are trying to spot errors linked to spelling or punctuation.

Colour coding

We have explored how colour in general can provide a vital tool for helping us to take control of our learning. Colour coding when proofreading is no exception. Using a traffic light system to colour code your work can provide a quick and easy way of identifying what still needs to be worked on. Use red to identify a word, phrase or paragraph that you want to come back to – this indicates that whilst the idea is good and you have captured the thought, the decoration still needs work:

- Highlighting in red will help you to keep track of those bits of your writing that you would like to revisit and develop.
- Orange can be used to highlight any words or phrases that still need a bit of refining or further polish before the work is finished.
- Green can be used to highlight words, phrases and paragraphs which you feel are fully developed, polished and are good to go! Using green in this way is also a very powerful way of boosting your motivation and helping you to see that you are progressing.

Colour coding could also be used to highlight that you have included all the right ingredients in your paragraphs – you can use colour to code your paragraphs and check these against the assignment brief or criteria to make sure that you have only made one concise point (e.g. Blue), have included some evidence (Purple) and have developed your point fully through your analysis or evaluation (Grey). Use the **PIES** strategy to help with this.

Student voices

‘As a lazy proofreader who often cuts this important step, I find the **Back to front reading** strategy particularly useful as it provides almost a fresh view of what I have written. If I read through my work chronologically, the chances of me picking up on errors I have made are slim. The **Colour coding** strategy is also useful as I initially find it hard to get my ideas down on the page. Knowing I can come back and edit using colours as a reminder is helpful.

Sam, BA Film Studies, UK ’

Find a friend

Swap your work with someone else and have an agreement that you will proofread each other's work. Reading someone else's work can also help you to spot things you could develop in your own writing, and your friend will spot mistakes in your work which you yourself might not have seen. Recognising the benefits of this approach can help us overcome any fear we may have of sharing our work with others.

The authors' approach to Welldoing

Although writing this book has not been a piece of cake, the **CAKE** strategy has certainly helped to make the writing process less overwhelming. We really tried to free ourselves up when writing by capturing our ideas on the page and not fixating on editing and tidying our sentences initially. Furthermore, we have now started using **CAKE** to manage everyday writing tasks, such as drafting a document for work or writing an email. The **Ideas freezer** has also provided us with a trusty go-to many a time. Our freezer is certainly full of lots of ideas stored for another day – who knows, we might have enough ideas for another book!

Key take aways

- Pay attention to the assignment brief so you can focus on its demands – are you going to need to show that you are adept at description, analysis or evaluation? Or does the assignment demand that you include a mixture of all of these as well as comparing and contrasting?

- Don't overdo it when you are shopping for the ingredients of your assignment – remember to use the **Shopping baskets** and **Shopping lists** approach to maximise the use of your time and work smarter not harder.

- Don't forget to make use of the **Ideas freezer** if you feel that you have found something useful but aren't sure whether you will definitely need it.

- Break down the task by using the recipe for **CAKE**, freeing up your thinking so that you focus in on one specific feature of your assignment, and help your paragraph structure by using the **PIES** recipe.

- When icing your cake and conducting the proofreading stage of your assignment, draw on strategies such as **Proofreading with purpose**, **Find a friend** and **Back to front reading** to ensure that the energy you use for proofreading is well spent.

My blank canvas

Use this space to make a note of strategies you think could be useful to help you make your planning and writing more effective. Remember to **Pick and mix**, **Develop your combo** and
Turn up (or down) the dial, so that you can personalise an approach that works for you.

Don't forget that you may find some of your favourite strategies from this chapter help you to apply **Welldoing4home** and **Welldoing4work**. Similarly, can any of the strategies you have selected be applied at a **Micro and macro** level? Could the strategies in this chapter be used to help you to save **Spoons**, and can you combine any of the strategies with our **Common sensory** approach?

Remember that you can also make a note of strategies from other chapters in this space – think outside the box and consider how other strategies from elsewhere in the book might also help you to make planning and writing a piece of cake!

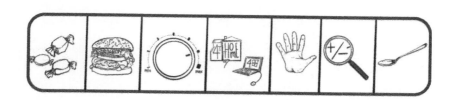

Further resources

- In order to make the most of the **Recipes for planning and writing** strategies, see the following templates in **Chapter 10**:

    o   Template 15: Cracking the recipe of assignment briefs and examination questions
    o   Template 16: Reading shopping baskets
    o   Template 17: Reading shopping lists
    o   Template 18: The ideas freezer

- The following resource from Cambridge Assessment International Education provides a useful introduction to the variety of command words you might come across in your assignment or exam questions: Understanding Command words in exams (cambridgeinternational.org): www.cambridgeinternational.org/exam-administration/what-to-expect-on-exams-day/command-words

- This guide from the University of Portsmouth explains what signposting is when essay writing and gives tips on how to use signposting to improve your written work: www.port.ac.uk/student-life/help-and-advice/study-skills/written-assignments/better-essays-signposting

- The following guidance produced by the University of Birmingham provides a number of useful tips for essay planning and writing: https://intranet.birmingham.ac.uk/as/libraryservices/library/asc/documents/public/short-guide-essay-planning.pdf

The revision elevator
Give your revision a lift!

Is this chapter for me?

- Do you struggle to plan and manage your revision?

- Are your 'go-to' revision strategies not as effective or successful as you would like?

- Do you overlook the need to spend time revising how you might use or apply the information you've committed to memory?

The revision elevator: The big picture

Revision can feel like one of the most stressful and pressured aspects of our learning; the stakes are high, time can feel like it is working against us and as the exams or assessment deadlines approach, the pressure and stress can begin to mount.

Revision often becomes habitual; we default to familiar approaches, such as re-reading and re-writing notes, and hope these will lead to success. However, the go-to strategies we adopt may not actually be the most effective or efficient for maximising our chances of retaining, recalling and applying as much knowledge of the topic as possible.

We also often think of revision as primarily being about committing things to memory. Whilst memorising content is an essential part of the revision process, if we overlook other equally important aspects of exam preparation, we may find we are not able to effectively retrieve this stored knowledge and apply it in a way that answers the question (in the language the examiner wants to see).

The **Revision elevator** chapter will therefore introduce you to a range of tried-and-tested revision strategies to boost and accelerate your ability to memorise information. It will also help you to improve your overall revision efficiency and effectiveness so that you get the biggest return on your investment, elevate your exam performance and increase your chances of success.

In this chapter, we will introduce you to a range of practical strategies to help you to:

- Put in the groundwork to ensure your revision is as impactful as possible (**Ground floor strategies**).
- Boost your ability to memorise and retrieve information via the **Memory elevator**.
- Elevate your assessment performance on the day with our top floor strategies (**Sky's the limit**).

Don't forget to think about how you can apply all of the different tools you have available to you from the **Welldoing toolkit** when you are considering the strategies in this chapter.

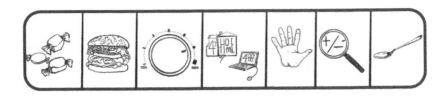

Ground floor strategies: Putting in the groundwork

Revision can feel like an infinite task with no obvious beginning or end. No matter how much revision we do, or how many times we revisit something, we can still end up feeling that we could have done more. Whilst it can be tempting to launch straight in and start revising, a little prior planning can really help you to take control of the process and maximise the impact of your revision. Before you hit the **Memory elevator** ascend button, spend a bit of time exploring our **Ground floor strategies** to help you get prepared. Ensuring you have done the groundwork will help you to get the most out of the Memory elevator and **Top floor strategies**, making your revision as effective as possible.

The grand plan!

Revision can seem like a daunting and endless task where the finish line is hard to visualise. Whilst creating a system for tracking your revision can seem like adding in an extra stage which takes you away from precious revision time, putting in place a way of managing, reviewing and tracking your progress from the start can help you to feel more in control. It is also useful for helping us to keep in mind the big picture and remember what we are working towards. Imagine you are planning a building. It is vitally important to put thought and effort into the planning stage so that it can be built effectively and efficiently. Outwardly, people see the results of the careful planning, but often forget the vital importance of the plans for the building's success. Revision is similar.

There are various ways of designing a tracking or mapping system. The key thing is to consider what your priorities are and how to put in place a system which will support your needs and help you to feel in control. Remember, the system you put in place should help you to see progress and feel like you are achieving. Be creative and use a system that supports and motivates you rather than overwhelms or undermines you. Also, don't be afraid to adapt or change your approach if it's really not working for you.

Here are a few things you might like to consider before you put together your own tailored system for tracking your revision.

Break it down

Breaking down subjects into bitesize chunks helps us to make a seemingly mammoth task, like revision, much more manageable. By breaking the task down, we are better able to plan how we can carry out each step in a sustainable way. This can be particularly useful when you are juggling numerous and often discrete topics within a subject.

This approach also helps us to recognise the overall size and shape of a subject, helping us to get a sense of how different topics are linked together or organised.

For example, rather than planning to revise a whole topic in Biology such as 'Genetics', consider what the subtopics are within that larger topic. Perhaps there were different lectures or experiments that you conducted that all contributed to the overall topic, but could be focused in on to break the topic down into more manageable chunks. The key is to then make sure you plan enough revision sessions to dedicate time to each aspect of the whole topic.

Bear in mind

A potential danger with the **Break it down** strategy is that you start to see the content of your revision as separated, siloed and unconnected. Make sure you take time to reflect on the connections between each of the different chunks that you have identified. Remember that these links can be within or even between different topics. See the **Interleaving** strategy further on in this chapter.

There's more to revision than just memorising

We often primarily think of preparing for an exam or a test as a memory-related task. However, the revision process is made up of several different stages that can be easy to overlook. Just as we can break down the topics themselves, we can also break down the *stages* of revision we would like to focus on. Therefore, consider whether you would like to track your memorising, understanding and/or applying to help you prioritise the type of revision-related activity you would like to focus on and track (see Figure 7.1). Often, if we really do understand something, it becomes easier to memorise.

Try using a table to keep track of the stages of revision, regularly updating the table to see how much progress you have made across these stages. You could also use colour, percentages or emojis to indicate how confident you feel about each area. See our **Revision elevator – Putting in the groundwork** template in **Chapter 10 (Template 19)**.

Areas to prioritise

Naturally, we tend to want to keep revisiting the bits of learning that we know or which have become 'cemented'. This is because it makes us feel good – it is familiar and by going back over it repeatedly, we gain a feeling of reassurance and our

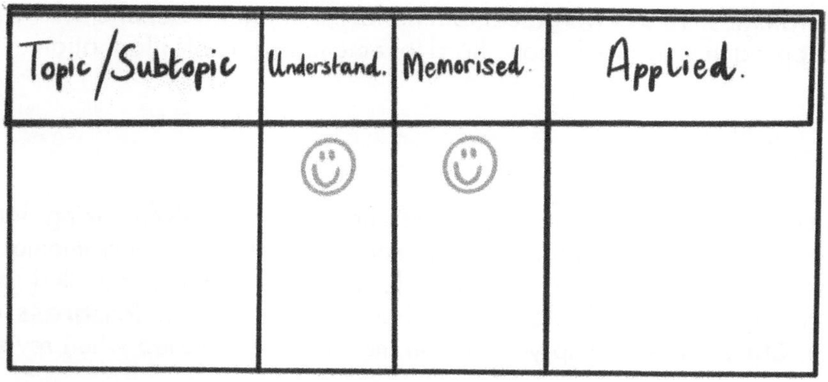

Topic/Subtopic	Understand.	Memorised.	Applied.
	☺	☺	

Figure 7.1   The different stages of revision

CAPTION: Table for tracking revision.

confidence is boosted. However, revision is often time-pressured so we need to be careful not just to keep revisiting the stuff that is firmly cemented at the expense of the other things we need to know, understand and be able to do. This aspect of tracking helps us to identify those areas of revision which are a priority.

You could combine this strategy with **There's more to revision than just memorising** above by looking at the rating you have given to each topic or subtopic and the stage of revision you're at. You can then plan the next stages of your revision, considering which areas need most attention and therefore more time. Taking stock like this helps you to adapt and respond smartly and flexibly to your revision needs – don't just stick to your original revision plan if you find that it won't help you to focus in on key areas. It may be that you need more time for one area and less time for another. Don't forget to refer to our **Manage your time rather than your time managing you** template in **Chapter 10 (Template 2)**.

The odd one out

It is also important to acknowledge that some things are easy for us to remember and some things seem to be much harder to cement – this doesn't always correlate with the difficulty of the material itself or how important it is to remember something! If you look for memory hot spots – those bits that no matter what you do, they simply won't stick – you can prioritise these as you'll likely need a little bit more time, effort and maybe multiple memory strategies to get them into your long-term memory. As a general rule, the harder something is to memorise, the more likely you are to need to go further up the revision elevator (see the **Memory Elevator**) and combine multiple strategies. This is where combining levels might be beneficial – we can use multiple approaches to crack those hard-to-remember bits of information.

An ending in sight

Tracking can also be used to help us to see our progress. Actively taking note of how we are moving in the right direction and keeping check on our incremental progress help to boost our motivation. It helps us to focus on the distance travelled rather than solely focusing on the work that we still have to do. See our **Progress checker** strategy in **Chapter 3** to help you to note the distance travelled when revising.

Check in on your Welldoing...
Revision progress checker

For this Check in, refer to our template on the **Revision elevator – Putting in the groundwork (Template 19)** in **Chapter 10**.
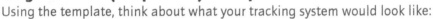   Using the template, think about what your tracking system would look like:

- How will you break down the task and topics of revision into more manageable chunks?
- How will you monitor the progress of your revision across different skills – understanding, memory retrieval, application?

Comfy revision

As discussed in **Cognitively Comfy Learning** in **Chapter 2**, our environment can be instrumental in shaping and influencing our ability to learn. How we experience our environment via our senses can impact on our cognitive as well as physical comfort and directly influence our concentration, motivation and stamina. When planning and preparing for your revision, consider your environment and where you will be most 'comfortable' to carry this out. Remember to personalise and tailor your approach to managing your environment so that your revision is as effective as possible.
  Consider whether you can:

Move (Chapter 2) in order to ensure you revise in an environment that is best suited to your needs, whether this is working in a quiet space, in a coffee shop or outside. Remember, everyone's 'ideal' environment will be different.

If you cannot move, consider how you might be able to better **Manage (Chapter 2)** your surroundings by adapting your environment based on the sensory triggers which affect you most, such as light, noise, smell and textures.

You may find it useful to also consider how **Micro-managing (Chapter 2)** your environment may help to boost the effectiveness of your revision. This is particularly important if you feel you have limited choice in terms of where you can work or how much you can control your environment.

Bear in mind

The **Micro-manage** strategies may also be very useful in the exam or test itself; don't underestimate the impact small tweaks can make to your exam performance.

Time and task savvy revision

Being time and task savvy is one of the most important factors in determining how effective your overall approach to revision will be. It is not uncommon for us to put together a revision timetable and then find that a few days (or even hours) in, we have to deviate from the plan or give up on it entirely! Putting together a revision timetable or plan which provides you with some routine and structure whilst also maintaining a degree of flexibility is really important.

We explore a range of strategies to help you to put together a flexible, tailored timetable which will support you to revise but in a way that is tailored to your needs and conflicting demands.

Take a look at the **Blocking out time** strategy (**Chapter 3**) to help you ensure your revision timetable takes note of any other events or commitments (study, work and life related) you need to juggle. This strategy can also help you to reflect on the times of day or week when you feel your revision may be most effective, such as first thing in the morning, or at the weekend.

Have a look at the **Buffer time** strategy (**Chapter 3**) to help you build a flexible revision plan which isn't set in stone. The Buffer time strategy will help you take into account changes in your mood or motivation levels whilst also enabling you to alter when you revise if you suddenly need to free up time for something else.

The **Chunk time** strategy (**Chapter 3**) can help you work out how you might like to best use the time you have set aside for revising. Consider whether you have a preference for short revision bursts or for longer revision sessions. Again, remember there is no ideal. It is also possible to include different lengths of 'chunks' depending on the revision-related task you are carrying out.

Stolen time (Chapter 3) is a strategy that is particularly important when planning your revision time as it can help you to recognise that revision can be incredibly effective when carried out for very short and intensive bursts. Could you make the most of the kettle boiling or whilst waiting for the bus to steal a few moments for some focused revision?

In addition to the strategies outlined in **Chapter 3**, the following may help you to ensure your revision is as effective as possible.

Flexible retrieval

When we learn, we can sometimes become creatures of habit. We may find we are naturally drawn to revisit the content we are revising in the same order. Whilst this can provide a greater sense of certainty and predictability to our revision, it can also undermine the impact of the revision. Try mixing up the order of topics when you revise as this will help your brain to make more connections. If you are using questions to self-test, you might also like to adapt the questions you pose for yourself as this will help to consolidate the effective and flexible retrieval of key information and knowledge.

Two (or more!) minds are better than one

Teaching or explaining your revision notes to someone else helps to cement key concepts or ideas. It also helps you to practise both retrieving the information from your memory and expressing this clearly to relay your point succinctly in a way that makes sense. See if there is an opportunity to learn with someone else, e.g. fellow students, friends, family members or even the family pet!

Interleaving

Forgetting and then having to remember something strengthens your memory and capacity to retrieve information. So, when you are revising, it can be really helpful to factor in time to move away from a topic and forget it. In a single revision session, try moving from one unrelated task or topic to another, before returning to the original topic. This is known as interleaving (Weinstein et al., 2018). It can also be a useful tool for helping you to make links between seemingly unrelated topics.

Also think about spacing out how often you revisit a topic. It might be that you find something quite difficult initially so taking a break from that topic and then revisiting it later might help to cement it. Then try extending the length of time that passes before you revisit it again. Perhaps return to it after one hour, then after a day, then after a whole week and gradually increase the length of the gap between revisits.

Bear in mind

Whilst moving between subjects can really help with effective retrieval, be careful not to keep jumping wildly from one subject to another so that your revision becomes disjointed or disconnected. Moving backwards and forwards between a couple of topics will be more effective as you will be creating the right conditions for effective interleaving.

The memory elevator: Strategies for boosting memory and recall

Some information seems to stick in our brains straight away, whilst other information can seem impossible to process, store and then recall. Furthermore, there is not always any obvious pattern to this. Adopting a multi-levelled approach to elevate your memory's capacity to store and retrieve information will boost the effectiveness of your revision.

The memory elevator introduces you to a range of strategies to boost your memory, but also encourages you to think of the different 'levels' you might need to engage with to revise successfully. Sometimes we might only need to visit one level of the revision elevator and the information sticks straight away. However, if you are struggling to remember something, rather than feeling like you have hit a wall, remember to get back into the elevator and head to another level.

Also remember that the elevator can go in two directions so feel free to move up and down as needed; you can revisit a level or combine some of the levels for those tricky bits of information that just won't stick. Engaging more fluidly in our revision and visiting different levels via the memory elevator can help us to successfully commit information to memory in a way that we can then locate, access and recall it when needed.

Level 1: Less is more

If you were heading off to the shops and needed to remember some key items you need to buy, you would probably not choose to write a whole side of written notes in full sentences – common sense would remind us that a list format would be far more powerful as a memory aide and ensure we don't forget any items. Similarly, whilst it can be reassuring to write our revision notes in full sentences, finding ways to reduce and streamline our notes will not only mean that it takes less time to make them, but also it will ultimately strengthen our memory. See our section on **Taking note of how we take notes: Strategies for effective note-taking** in **Chapter 5** for more strategies on making impactful revision notes.

You may like to use a form of shorthand to save you time and further streamline the process. You might like to invent your own shorthand words for key terms linked to the content you need to remember, or you might find that you can use shorthand terms, abbreviations or acronyms which already exist for your subject.

You could also limit yourself to using a certain number of words so that you have to actively process the information you are converting into revision notes, reducing the chance that you passively copy it from one place to another.

Level 2: Bitesize revision

For each revision session, think about how you will break down and chunk the information into manageable bitesize pieces that will be easier to commit to memory than a huge amount of information. This links in some ways to how you have broken down your revision topics in the **Ground level** section above, but is also about how you manage the information *within* a revision session. For example, try using flash cards or sticky notes to chunk information. Chunking in this way sets you smaller goals to work towards and supports your memory's capacity to process and retain information.

Level 3: A picture paints a thousand words

This level considers visual cues and dual coding, which often helps to support memory (Caviglioli, 2022).

If you make multiple revision cards and aids which look similar, this can reduce memory efficiency. When streamlining your notes, try and get into the habit of presenting them in a way that makes them look different to each other. Using a mixture of bullet points, mind maps, flow charts, diagrams and any other way you can think of will boost your memory's capacity. Try and use revision spaces differently; for example, if you are using flashcards, try to arrange information in different formats so that when you revisit the topic your brain will have a much better chance of recalling the information quickly as it is linked to the 'shape' and 'look' of the content.

Dual coding is another powerful strategy to support memory retrieval (Clark and Paivio, 1991). An image, drawing or diagram used to accompany an idea or some written words can boost your memory's capacity. Not only does this reduce the chance of all your revision aides looking identical, it provides a powerful memory trigger or memory hook and helps you to visualise the content.

Level 4: Numbering technique

Numbering can also boost your memory's capacity. As an example, if you have a revision aide with several bullet points you need to remember for a certain concept, by counting and noting the total number of points you need to remember, you can give yourself an additional safety net or memory trigger.

Level 5: Colour

Colour is a powerful tool to boost memory and retrieval; it can be used to highlight significant bits of information or to indicate a pattern that might help us to memorise more information. Try using different colours to ensure your revision cards look and 'feel' different from one another. You can also use colour when revisiting your revision to highlight those bits that are harder to memorise or simply won't stick. Colour can be used in a wide range of different ways. This will maximise your chances of helping your brain retrieve the right information when needed.

Level 6: Lost your train of thought

Linked learning and pattern recognition can be great tools for boosting memory. We tend not to remember things in isolation – we usually link something new, unfamiliar or abstract with something we already know (Bruner, 1996: 56). In a similar way, it is often easier to recall and remember something if we can see a pattern.

Sometimes patterns are obvious, for example the ten times table is easier to remember than the eight times table as there is an obvious pattern which helps us to link together the information. When revising, try looking for patterns in the information you are trying to make sense of. Note that some of the most challenging things to remember are hard because there is not an immediately obvious pattern. When this is the case, you can create artificial patterns to help you link information together.

Level 7: Same old story

You can use stories to cement memory. Putting what you are trying to remember into a story helps your brain to connect different ideas. You're then more likely to be able to remember the linked ideas compared to the individual parts on their own. Be creative and build a story that works for you.

Pause for thought

Why not try this strategy now. How could you link together the following items into a story?

Football

Banana

Dog

Hat

Cheese

Tree

Book

Level 8: Mnemonics

Often, we just need a very small prompt or starting point, such as a single letter, to help us to remember a word or phrase: these little letters can have a big impact! Mnemonics are great memory hooks that can allow us to remember names or sequences, such as the order of the planets from the Sun. Mnemonics are likely to be even more helpful if you create them yourself.

Level 9: Revision on the move

Movement can boost our thinking and processing and can provide a useful memory boost if you are finding it hard to make something stick (Madan and Singhal, 2012). You could try using certain hand movements and linking this to specific bits of information you need to retain. This is done in physics when using the right-hand rule to work out the direction of magnetic forces. Or perhaps record your revision and listen to this whilst going for a walk or a jog – remember that learning doesn't always have to be done when we are stationary. Some of our best thinking can be generated when we are on the move.

Level 10: Take a trip down memory lane

We have talked a lot throughout the book about the importance of environment in shaping our ability to study effectively. Our environment can also be harnessed to boost our revision and location can be used to enhance memory. For example, you may find it useful to place some of your revision resources at different locations around the house. This might take the form of making revision posters and arranging these in different rooms around the home, almost like a gallery, where you can move about and learn to associate different parts of a subject with different spaces in your home. You might also find it helpful to use location to boost language learning, sticking small memory aides to key items throughout the house to help you remember particular vocabulary. Some people also find it helpful to associate particular aspects of a topic they are trying to remember with special places or locations. For example, it might be helpful to link specific aspects of a subject you are memorising to the steps you take on a regular walk you do. Place can be very evocative and help us to cement new knowledge linked to somewhere we know.

Level 11: Building revision into a daily routine

As so much of your time is likely to be taken up with revising, consider aligning some of your revision tasks or topics with specific features linked to your daily routine. A revision poster or set of cards placed by the fridge, kettle or bathroom mirror can help to jog your memory when you revisit these spaces. Not only does this make the most of your time but it also supports your ability to recall information linked to specific settings or locations.

Level 12: Get gaming

Many resources now exist that help you to gamify your revision – or create your own! For example, you could play Pictionary, Taboo or try online quizzes. This is a much more active way to revise compared to, for example, watching a YouTube video or reading a revision guide. Flashcards lend themselves well to gamifying your revision and testing your memory – each card has two sides, making it perfect for flipping it over and hiding the content you need to test yourself on. This can work well when revising with others.

Student voices

When I first started A level Chemistry, I found the subject quite challenging and was struggling to achieve the grades I would have liked. Previously producing handwritten notes before exams had worked well for me as revision technique, but it didn't seem to be working as well anymore. So, I began developing a **Combo** of more interactive styles of revision, such as creating flash cards and mind maps. A key feature of these revision strategies which helped immensely with active recall in an exam situation was the colours used. I would often write key words or equations in colour which allowed me to physically visualise these key bits of information vividly in exams. This **Combo** of revision approaches really helped me to refine my chemistry knowledge and succeed in my exams.

Evie, A level student, UK

Sky's the limit: Top floor strategies

The end is almost in sight! You've made it up to the top of the building and hopefully saved some much-needed time and energy in the process by using the revision elevator rather than taking the stairs. One final push will now help you to ensure that all of the hard work that you have put into revising pays off. Explore the top floor strategies on the following pages, and, with a bit of final extra preparation and planning, you can ensure that the sky's the limit when it comes to your exam performance on the day.

Brain dump

When you start the exam, try writing down some of the key points or pieces of information to save you having to hold all the information in your head for the whole exam.

You can then refer back to these as you move through the paper. If other ideas come to you whilst writing, set aside a space where you can jot this down so you don't forget it and then return to what you were focusing on. See our **Ideas freezer** strategy in **Chapter 6** to help with this.

Revise 'how' to tackle the exam

We often make memory aides on the *topics* we need to cover but making some memory aides for the *processes* or *steps* we need to follow in the exam itself can also be helpful. For example, you might find it helpful to make some revision cards for key mathematical formulas you need to remember, or a useful formula for writing particular types of essay response. See our **PIES: The secret ingredients of paragraphs** recipe in **Chapter 6** for help with this.

If there are key things that you often forget in an exam, such as to spend a bit of time proofreading, then make a revision aides to remind you of this. You might even find it useful to make some revision aides to remind you to use some of the strategies in this book! Remember that revision should not just be about memorising content or subject knowledge, it should also be about memorising the skills, strategies and life-lines which might not only help us to give our best performance but also support us to manage nerves or unexpected setbacks.

Studying success

Look through practise papers, mark schemes and examiner reports. All of these are great sources of information that will help you gain an insight into what is expected of you, how you should set out your work, common topics that come up and areas of confusion. Looking at model answers can also help you to determine what success looks like; even looking at poorer answers can help you to understand what *not* to do. Make sure you work out what has made the answer successful, or not, so that you understand the why, rather than just 'what' you need to do. It can also be useful to look at mark schemes, examiner reports and model answers as a way to identify patterns in terms of where you might be dropping marks, giving you key pointers to focus on when in the exam. For example, do you often lose marks because you're not showing your working, or you forget to use certain key terms or words?

Create the scene and practise playing the part

Practise doing parts of the assessment in the way that you will need to carry it out on the day. For example, if you're preparing for an interview or live question and answer session, you could ask a friend to talk to you or quiz you so that you practise answering out loud. If you are doing an exam, set aside some time to complete an exam question under exam conditions with a timer so you start to get used to the environment you will be working in when you take the assessment. This can help you to build confidence and learn to navigate any setbacks that come up. Furthermore, if you have exam access arrangements, try to practise whilst drawing on the exam arrangements you know you are entitled to (Rodeiro and Macinska, 2022).

Coming to terms with new or unfamiliar terms

Sometimes unfamiliar words or references in a question, such as a term or word we haven't come across, an equation we are not familiar with or a chemical or organism we have never heard of, can really knock our confidence. This can lead to panic as we think that we can't do a question that has been set. If this happens, try to step back from the specific *context* of a question. Instead, think about the key *concepts* of the course and try to work out which of these the question or task is hoping that you will focus on.

A question of order

Although it can feel like we have very little control in an exam in terms of the questions we are asked, we can at least have a say in terms of what order we answer the questions in. It can be a good idea to go for any 'quick wins' or questions which you are potentially strong on first so you can bank those marks and boost your confidence in the process. Alternatively, you might find it is most helpful to tackle some of the trickier questions first, especially if there are more marks attached to these questions. The important thing is to tackle the questions in an order that works best for you.

Beating the clock

Paying attention to the total time you will have in the exam and chunking this can help with ensuring you can complete the examination. For example, you could divide time between questions so that if you get stuck on a question, you have set yourself a time limit to try to deal with it but then move to another after this time has passed. It is also wise to factor in a bit of buffer time in case your timings don't go to plan and you need to use some extra time to finish off a particular question. Don't forget that you are likely to need time to go back and check your answers so you don't lose marks by making silly mistakes.

Running out of time... When you feel like the clock is beating you

There is nothing worse than that sinking feeling when you know that time is running out and you haven't completed all the questions or written everything you wanted to. If you think you may run out of time in an exam, it can be useful to change your strategy. Before the exam, it often pays to have already thought about what the quick wins could be for your subject or exam format if you literally only had five minutes left. For example, rather than leaving a multiple-choice question blank, choose a letter – any letter – as it might just get you an extra mark! Could you write in bullet points rather than full sentences if that is slowing you down? Will using a labelled drawing help you explain something more quickly than writing about it? If you feel like you are running out of time, remember to brain dump any extra key words to bag a few extra marks. Thinking of strategies to deal with a lack of time BEFORE the exam helps you to have strategies you can draw on which you are unlikely to think of when under the pressure of an exam.

The clues are in the question

Teachers often repeatedly remind us to READ and ANSWER the question that has been set. In spite of this, it can be really easy to miss a vital clue or bit of information when reading questions at speed and under pressure in the exam. Practise responding to questions and retrieving the right information matched to the clues contained in the question and instructions, rather than regurgitating everything you know.

Try and also become familiar with the style of the paper you will be sitting. Spend time getting to know the language of the paper. See if there are any patterns, commonly missed clues, etc. If you are producing a longer answer, say in the form of an essay, make sure you pick out the key words in terms of *what* you are being asked to do such as analyse, evaluate, compare and so on. It can be useful to take a highlighter into the exam or some coloured pens and get into the habit of really paying attention to the key terms and of returning back to the question regularly to check you are still on track. Take a look at our **Unpicking the recipe of assignment briefs** in **Chapter 6** for further help on this.

Learn the examiner's language

Sometimes we can lose valuable marks for not using the discipline-specific terminology in an assessment. You may know the answer and have articulated it well, but if you have not used key words that the marker expects you to be using then this can be very frustrating if it causes you to lose marks. If you are preparing for a subject where the wording is vital to demonstrate your understanding and receive the marks then build this into your revision and make sure you not only practise recalling the information but that you also revise *communicating* this in the right way to ensure you don't drop unnecessary marks. Insights into this can be found from reading textbooks, others' exam answers, mark schemes, exemplar work from other students and listening to your teacher communicate with you. Use all of these sources to help you develop familiarity with the key words and language used in your discipline and practise adopting these words.

Student voices

'Revision is often associated with painstaking amounts of memorisation and re-writing notes in one sitting. The **Revision elevator** provided the perfect formula to get ahead with my revision. The **Ground floor** strategies helped me to build a blueprint to study smart, whereas the **Memory elevator** gave me tips to integrate these strategies into my daily routine. This was a gamechanger which helped me to avoid pre-exam panic.

Gayathri, MSc in Molecular Biosciences, India '

Plan B: Preparing for the unexpected

Although this might not sound like the most obvious way of approaching exam preparation, it can be really helpful to revise what to do when things don't go to plan. We tend to practise what we should do when things go right, but sometimes by spending a bit of time revising some Plan B approaches we can boost our confidence by knowing that we will be able to manage any challenges or setbacks that arise. For example, you could practise what to do if time runs out – it might sound counter-intuitive but setting a clock with less time and seeing how you manage the process of time running out might be an invaluable lesson to practise in a safe way so that if this then does happen in the actual exam you know how to tackle it. Or you might find it helpful to practise steps to go through if you experience a wave of panic – what strategies could you draw on as Plan B if you need to manage your anxiety levels in the exam setting? What about if your memory goes blank – this is quite normal and a very common occurrence but it can be scary. What could you do to actively take control in this situation?

The common sensory approach to exams

Don't forget that whilst we can't always control when and where we will be situated for an exam, we can still make very small adaptions to how we experience our environment such as wearing clothing we feel comfortable in, taking off our shoes, or fiddling with a bracelet to create a sensation of movement. Revisit the **Micromanage** strategies in **Chapter 3**.

Bear in mind

If you're worried about trialling a new strategy and it is not working so well for you, try it out in a low-stakes environment first, such as a mock exam, in-class work or practise interview. At least then if it doesn't work so well, you have the chance to switch strategy for the final assessment. You can even try it in a non-study environment such as practising revision and retrieval of birthdays or your to-do list.

The authors' approach to Welldoing

With busy lives, we can all feel like we have a lot of info we need to retain. Whilst we no longer have to use the revision elevator for exam preparation, we do still have our favourite 'levels' which we use if we have to remember some key info, whether it's for doing the food shopping or presenting without notes. Karen always uses **Level 4** – the numbering technique – to help  her remember how many things she needs to take with her when she leaves the house; Loti often uses **Level 3** images to paint a mental picture of things she needs to remember; and Abby uses **Level 6** pattern recognition to memorise new information at work and link ideas together. If, for any reason, one of our go to 'levels' is not working for us, we get back in that elevator and whizz to another floor to help us cement things in our brains.

My blank canvas

Use this space to make a note of strategies you think could be useful to help you give your revision a lift. Remember to **Pick and mix**, **Develop your combo** and **Turn up (or down) the dial**, so that you can personalise an approach that works for you.

Don't forget that you may find some of your favourite strategies from this chapter help you to apply **Welldoing4home** and **Welldoing4work**. Similarly, can any of the strategies you have selected be applied at a **Micro and macro** level? Could the strategies in this chapter be used to help you to save **Spoons**, and can you combine any of the strategies with our **Common sensory** approach?

Remember that you can also make a note of strategies from other chapters in this space – think outside the box and consider how other strategies from elsewhere in the book might help to boost your revision so that the sky's the limit!

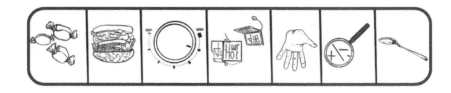

Key take aways

- Effective revision consists of different skills and approaches that complement one another.

- Lay the ground work using the **Ground floor** strategies such as establishing the grand plan, getting comfy with your revision environment and being savvy with the tasks you have to complete and the time you have to do it in.

- Then move through the different levels of the **Memory elevator** to boost your memory and recall in a way that suits you and meets your needs. You might start at **Level 1: Less is more**, then move on to **Level 4: Numbering technique**, though could need to go back to **Level 2** or combine levels if you find that your approach isn't working so well in the beginning.

- Don't forget the **Top floor** strategies where you can practise and hone your exam technique through strategies such as **Brain dump**, **Studying success** and **A question of order**. Remember to think about how you will make sure you are cognitively comfy in your exam environment too.

Further resources

- In order to make the most of the **Revision elevator** strategies, see the following templates in **Chapter 10**:

  - Template 2: Managing your time rather than your time managing you
  - Template 19: Revision elevator: putting in the groundwork

- This resource gives more information on the spacing approach that can help to boost memory: www.retrievalpractice.org/spacing

- This podcast explains interleaving in more detail: www.learningscientists.org/learning-scientists-podcast/2017/12/6/episode-8-interleaving

- This set of webpages from the Open University includes videos and tips to help you reflect on your exam technique: https://help.open.ac.uk/exam-techniques

- The students on this webpage are in their final year of school and they share great tips on making revision work for you, drawing on a number of the revision elevator **Ground floor** strategies: www.bbc.co.uk/bitesize/articles/zn3497h

- Medical professionals — as discussed in the Prologue, this book is not a therapeutic book. Its aim is to act as a preventative toolkit, so we strongly encourage you to reach out for professional and medical help should you find yourself in a position where anxiety is affecting your ability to prepare for or carry out exams.

Walking a tightrope

The safety net approach to thriving rather than surviving when public speaking

Is this chapter for me?

- Do you dread the thought of any public speaking, whether informal or formal?

- Do you find that you spend lots of time memorising everything you need to say to put your mind at ease?

- Do the logistics of presenting, such as when, where and how you will present overwhelm you?

Walking a tightrope: The big picture

One of the most common aspects of study which students frequently dread is the prospect of having to speak publicly in front of others, whether doing a presentation or speaking in front of a group. When we produce work over a longer period of time, in the form of a project or portfolio, we have the safety net of knowing that we can check our work multiple times before we submit it. When faced with the task of public speaking, this safety net vanishes as we lose the ability to edit our performance before it goes public.

Consequently, even just the thought of public speaking can push us firmly outside of our comfort zone. We might liken this feeling to walking a tightrope where we are suddenly exposed, vulnerable or 'on show', having to perform in front of our peers. We fear that we could falter and tumble at any moment; this feeling of a high chance of 'failure', 'getting it wrong' or embarrassing ourselves with no way out often leads to increased stress, anxiety and nerves. It therefore comes as no surprise that the fear of public speaking is often considered the most common phobia ahead of snakes or heights (British Council, 2022)! Even if you dislike public speaking, it is still possible to be good at it and you may find that over time it becomes more doable. Likewise, if you never get to the point where you fully enjoy public speaking or presenting, there are lots of safety net strategies which you can employ to reduce the fear factor and help make the process much more manageable.

Walking a tightrope provides an honest exploration of the challenges of public speaking and presenting. Each of the strategies can be considered as a safety net, helping to boost your confidence; the safety net strategies are largely transferable to a range of public speaking contexts such as seminars, vivas, group presentations, interviews, as well as one-on-one speaking. Remember to select the safety net strategies which are most useful to you and applicable to your particular situation.

In this chapter, we will introduce you to a range of practical strategies to help you to:

- Develop faith that you can navigate the tightrope of public speaking by putting in place a range of **Safety net strategies**.
- Build your confidence so that you feel able to move away from rote memorisation of your presentation and **Going off script** without feeling you are going to fall.
- Anticipate and plan for common logistical challenges associated with presenting to reduce anxiety and stress (**Plan B**).
- Harness your environment to increase your control and comfort when public speaking (**Comfy presenting**).

Don't forget to think about how you can apply all of the different tools you have available to you from the **Welldoing toolkit** when you are considering the strategies in this chapter.

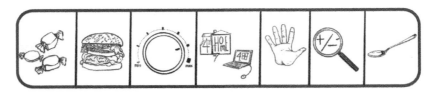

Check in on your Welldoing...
What's the root of our anxiety around presenting?

When we find that we are nervous about public speaking or presenting, we often view this as a singular problem. But actually, the cause of our nerves is likely to be made up of many different elements which all happen to come together when we are asked to speak publicly.

Consider which of the following aspects of speaking in public are particular triggers for you:

- All attention is on me. I am in the spotlight.
- If I outwardly look nervous and uncomfortable, people will notice and will see through my acting to look confident.
- I might forget what I am saying. I won't look professional.
- I might not be able to answer a question if I am put on the spot. I'll look stupid.
- If I present in an unfamiliar environment, I won't know how to work the technology, how the room will be set up or what the room will look like.
- I find it worse presenting or speaking in front of people I know and fear their judgment more than presenting to people I don't know.
- I get anxious when I have to speak to a very large group of people. The pressure is high in this environment.
- I really dislike doing one-to-one presentations or presenting to small groups of people. It is really intense.
- It's not the actual presenting that increases my stress levels, but it's all the preparation and planning that go alongside it, such as knowing where I need to be, what time I should get there and how I will get there. I will be exhausted before I even start.

Try to pinpoint the specific aspects of public speaking which create additional stress for you as this will help you to choose the appropriate **Safety net strategies** to help you address these. Don't worry if there are multiple things you are worrying about – this is quite normal. Remember to **Pick and mix** a range of strategies which can be combined together as this will enable you to simultaneously manage and reduce the multiple stressors that you experience.

Safety net strategies

As mentioned, presenting and public speaking often rank as one of people's greatest fears. You are therefore definitely not alone if the thought of standing up and getting on the public speaking tightrope makes you feel on edge or like running in the opposite direction. The Safety net strategies shared next will support you to actively anticipate and mitigate the common challenges experienced when faced with the prospect of public speaking. They aim to allow you to regain a sense of control and support you to develop the confidence to take your first steps onto the public speaking tightrope. Use our **Safety net approach to presenting and public speaking** template in **Chapter 10** to help you get started (**Template 21**).

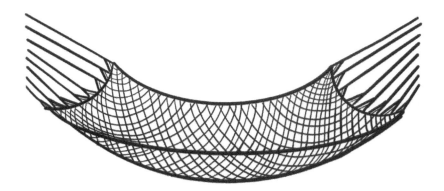

Harness your nervous energy

We often identify stress as a problem and something to avoid. In fact, a certain level of stress or pressure is not only normal but, ironically, can help us to perform by boosting our focus, motivation and energy. The trick is to learn to *harness* this nervous energy. Next time you get that dreaded feeling of butterflies in your stomach, sweaty palms or shortness of breath, remind yourself that rather than trying to undermine and ruin your performance, the nerves you are experiencing may well in fact help you to focus and deliver. It is also worth noting that whilst we may be painfully aware of our hands shaking or voice wobbling, others will not have the same awareness. Even if you worry others will see your nervousness, this does not undermine the strength of your presentation; this can show that you care, that you are invested and that you are real and human. Presenting is not about appearing to be perfect; it is about trying to connect with your audience. Therefore, although it may feel uncomfortable, try not to fight and extinguish your fear but accept it is there and work with it.

(Dis)Connecting with the audience

Depending on your preference, you may find connecting with your audience or peers helps to put you at ease. For example, speaking with someone in the room before the session starts or saying 'hello' to people in the room can help you to build a connection with the group and remove some of the 'formality' associated with public speaking. But if you feel that this will increase your nerves and make the situation more difficult, you don't need to interact with others in this way and you can try instead to keep disconnected from them. For example, it might help to focus on a point in the distance rather than looking at everyone's faces or focus on getting your slides or resources organised.

Practise (in all its forms) makes perfect

You can also build up your confidence with public speaking incrementally. Rather than simply considering rehearsing for a specific presentation as the only way to practise, see if you can identify different opportunities to 'practise' speaking in public more generally, such as asking or answering a question in class, to get used to hearing your own voice out loud. Public speaking is not something we can always crack overnight, therefore set yourself very small and gradual goals to work towards to develop your confidence over time and in a way that feels comfortable to you. When doing a more formal presentation, taking the opportunity to practise before you present can help you build confidence. Try seeking feedback from someone you trust. It's also not just about practising words for the presentation – perhaps you can practise projecting your voice, or how you will stand etc.

Student voices

‘Public speaking has always been something I've feared – all eyes on me, listening and watching. From the **Safety net** strategies, I have learnt that practising in different scenarios and familiarising myself with my own voice helps combat this fear and therefore allows me to manage the anxiety a little more.

Daisy, BA English Language and Linguistics, UK ’

Pre and post presenting 'buffer'

If possible, try not to schedule other things right up to and immediately after the presentation. Make a bit of time for yourself beforehand to allow you to prepare. Set aside some time after the presentation to decompress and acknowledge your accomplishment. Perhaps you can treat yourself in some way. If you can't do this straight away due to other commitments, then remember to reward yourself later.

Dreaded questions

It can be scary to know that you will be asked questions after you have completed a presentation or within a group seminar or discussion. However, you can prepare for this aspect to an extent by guessing the type of questions you might be asked. Remember to make the most of thinking time – you don't need to answer straight away. The silence before you respond will feel much longer to you than it does to those awaiting a response. Don't feel like you have to provide a perfect answer to every question asked either – you could use a **Dreaded question** to generate discussion and ask others their opinion.

All in good time

Try to arrive in good time before the start of your presentation. This will not only reduce any unnecessary pressure associated with finding the room and being there on time, but will give you a bit more time to familiarise yourself with your environment. You will have time to check the technology setup, load up your presentation and make any adaptions to the environment that will help to put you at ease such as adjusting lights, windows etc. See **Chapter 2** on **Cognitively comfy learning**. If you are particularly worried about the build-up to a presentation and find this in fact is causing more nerves than the presentation itself, then it can be useful to spend time planning for the logistics before the presentation. This might include visiting the environment you will be presenting in before the day/time of the presentation (or doing this virtually if you can't do this in person), planning your route or checking public transport timings.

Dress for success!

Whether we are public speaking in front of an audience or as part of an interview, how we physically present ourselves can impact how we feel. Spend a little time thinking about what you will wear. You might like to consider how the clothes you choose make you look (e.g. professional, appropriate for the setting) but you may also like to think about your cognitive comfort. Select clothes and shoes that you feel comfortable in, but which also boost your confidence.

Don't despair!

As we have said, public speaking can be challenging for everyone, but this is often not permanent and the chances are it will get easier with time as your confidence grows.

That said, if you feel overwhelmed at the thought of having to speak publicly or present and are not sure how to manage this, especially if this is an essential part of your studies, then make sure you let your teachers know. They will be able to work with you and signpost you to additional support for exploring ways to make this aspect of your study more manageable for you. Remember that you do not need to problem-solve this on your own; others will be able to support you in this and find a way forward.

Student voices

‘ As a fresh Master's student, I have first-hand experience trying to juggle study, exams and job interviews all at the same time. I found the **Safety net strategies** very useful and applicable not only in study but also in interviews which is the most important moment to show what we have learnt and could contribute to the company. While my weakness is long-script reciting which demonstrates insufficient interactions with the interviewers due to nervousness, the strategies helped me to understand that presenting or public speaking is not as hard as we think. There are little but significant changes that can have a positive impact on the way that we present to make it smoother and stress-free. If you are having the same problem as me, please do not hesitate to read them through! ’

Zach, MSc Sustainability and Management, Hong Kong

Going off script: Flexible presenting

We tend to associate presenting with perfection. Because of the lack of control associated with presenting, people understandably sometimes try to compensate for this by memorising a scripted version of their presentation. Whilst this seems like a logical approach to take, and certainly helps to reduce the fear factor of presenting, it is not always helpful in the long run.

Remember, presenting is not about memorising or reading a word-perfect script, but rather it is about our ability to engage with our audience. Although this may initially sound scary, what this means in reality is that our performance does *not* need to be perfect; some great presentations include mistakes, but this doesn't detract from the presentation and, counter-intuitively, it can actually make it more human and relatable.

That said, it can feel like we are removing a safety net when we remove the certainty which a 'script' appears to provide. However, by being more flexible with the way in which we approach and prepare for presentations, we can ironically gain more control over the process and actively plan for bumps in the road. The following Safety net strategies will help you to practise the art of flexible presenting:

- Rather than trying to write a script in full, brief notes in the form of cards or a diagram can give a much-needed memory prompt. Images can help to prompt memory too if you are worried about forgetting what you want to say. For example, include well-chosen images on presentation slides to help your audience to take on board your ideas whilst also acting as a content reminder for yourself. These can be helpful if you lose your train of thought, acting like a safety net to return back to.
- When making notes, focus on the bits of the presentation that you are likely to find most tricky or difficult to commit to memory; often the first few sentences are the hardest. It can sometimes be useful to highlight key points on your notes or use colour to help keep in sight the trickier bits of the presentation. Knowing that you have taken steps to help you navigate the more challenging parts of your presentation can be a reassuring safety net.
- If you want to practise your presentation, try to practise recalling the key points rather than every single word in a script. For example, perhaps focus your memory on the key points that you need to make or the points which you know are going to be the trickiest, almost like a prioritised script.

Student voices

‘The prospect of speaking in front of an audience has always scared me. It feels close to an analogy of engaging in a constant obstacle race. Not only have I applied the idea of **Pick and mixing** strategies when I am presenting, but I have also focused on **Going off script** and preparing for **Dreaded questions**. Making a **Combo** from these two opposing strategies has helped me engage fully with the audience, balancing the idea of a script and the freedom the lack of it provides.

Mimi, PhD student, Romania ’

Plan B

Taking some time to think about the most likely challenges that you might face when presenting can actually help you to better anticipate and plan for how you could overcome the challenges if they did actually happen, rather than this increasing your anxiety. You can't anticipate everything but being prepared in advance allows you to feel more in control. However, don't overdo it and prepare for every tiny and *unlikely* scenario – this will waste your time and energy.

Here are some things you might like to think about:

- **Internet connection:** If you are going to be presenting online, make sure to check your internet connection. Have a backup plan for if you lose connection and share this with someone else so they know what to do.

- **Interruptions:** If you are worrying about background interruptions, such as your dog barking or noisy roadworks from the street, sometimes acknowledging this by making a joke of it and apologising to people (before it happens!) can help to take the pressure off.
- **Tech check:** Both in person and online, it can be helpful to run a quick tech check before you present. Check your microphone and video. Can you be seen and heard? Importantly, can you hear others too? Are your slides advancing? Is the pointer working? You can also send your slides to someone else who will be at the presentation in advance so that you know that your slides can be shared if, for some reason, you are not able to share them yourself. Emailing them to yourself can also be a very handy backup.
- **Running out of time:** See if there are natural points in your presentation where you can miss out a section or skip over something if you are running out of time. You can also build in additional material which you can use if needed and the time is available, knowing that this can be skipped if you need to move on.
- **Late arrival:** Sometimes, no matter how meticulously we plan our journey or how much extra time we leave, something happens that is beyond our control and we realise we are going to be late. In this case, make sure you know who you will call to let them know. Explain what has happened and give an update of your estimated arrival time. Remember to keep your contact up to date if your estimated arrival time changes.

Bear in mind

You're unique – it would be boring if everyone presented in the same way. This is why it is important to work out what works for you. Remember that when you are public speaking, you as a person are not being assessed, but rather the way you are able to adapt to the situation and the audience is what matters most.

Comfy presenting

Remember that by being more mindful of our environment and its impact on us, we can actually increase our control and make ourselves more 'comfortable' when speaking publicly. Some example comfy safety net strategies are shared below.

Put on the spot!

There is something quite scary and unnatural about speaking in a room full of people where all eyes are focused on us – it can feel like we are literally being put on the spot. Find out if there is flexibility in where you can position yourself. For example, if you're doing a presentation, would you prefer to be sitting, standing still or moving about when you present? Some people find standing behind a lectern or table less nerve wracking whereas others prefer to stand in front of it. If you're in a seminar, what position in the room will you be most comfortable? Do you prefer to be at the front or back of the room, or do you prefer to be sat next to others or with some space around you?

Movement

If you are about to do a presentation, think about whether moving around could help you to harness your nerves. We often think that presenting is something that is static, but a little bit of movement around the room can help you to better interact with your audience and manage your nerves. Movement can also aid your thinking and ability to communicate. If you'd like to move whilst presenting, consider using an electronic pointer to free you from the computer if you are using slides. Movement can also help to get rid of adrenaline, which can reduce anxiety.

Mini-movements

If you find movement is very beneficial to helping manage your nerves or focus your thinking, you may also like to consider whether mini-movements could be useful, particularly if you find yourself in a situation where you are not able to move around freely, such as in an interview or a seminar. Little movements like using your hands to gesture to slides, tapping your foot, fiddling with a pen or bottle of water (if not distracting or obvious to others), wiggling your toes in your shoes or pushing your feet into the floor can help to make you feel more grounded and recreate the sensation of movement that aids your thinking and reduces your nerves.

All eyes *not* on you

If you are worried about the feeling of everyone's attention being focused solely on you, try using slides or images to support your presentation. Having images or diagrams which visually support the points you are making can refocus the audience's eye towards the slide, rather than all eyes being focused on you. In this and other contexts, asking questions and encouraging others to participate can also deflect some attention away from you as the speaker so that you don't feel under the spotlight for the whole duration of the presentation. This also helps to make the session more interactive and engaging, particularly when you're delivering a presentation, which is an added bonus!

Alternate focus

Having a bottle of water or a sweet (such as a cough sweet that you can suck) can provide you with something to focus on beyond the fact that you are speaking publicly. This can help to reduce nerves. It may be possible to have a hot drink with you to help you to relax. Reflect on what you think might provide you with an alternate focus before the session, interview or presentation is scheduled and check to see what is possible.

The authors' approach to Welldoing

We all have to do public speaking as part of our jobs, so it is something we are all used to. But that does not always mean we love it! We all recognise that how we feel changes and while we might feel really up to presenting or speaking publicly on one day or in a particular context, this is not always the case; we all have those days where we would rather hide away or we worry more about not presenting well or showing ourselves up in front of our peers. The strategies in this chapter have therefore proved invaluable and we often **Pick and mix** a range of strategies to build our own **Combo**. **Plan B** and **Comfy presenting** are some of our firm favourites!

Key take aways

- You can get more comfortable with public speaking by employing a range of **Safety net** strategies.

- By checking in on your own feelings about public speaking, you may find that the Welldoing strategies for **(Dis)Connecting with the audience** and **Dreaded questions** help to ease your anxiety, or it could be that building in a **Pre and post presenting 'buffer'** combined with **All in good time** help to keep you calm.

- The environment is key when you are presenting – take note of the **Comfy presenting** strategies to take account of the impact your presenting environment has on you.

My blank canvas

Use this space to make a note of strategies you think could be useful to help make you feel more comfortable with presenting. Remember to **Pick and mix**, **Develop your combo** and **Turn up (or down) the dial**, so that you can personalise an approach that works for you.

Don't forget that you may find some of your favourite strategies from this chapter help you to apply **Welldoing4home** and **Welldoing4work**. Similarly, can any of the strategies you have selected be applied at a **Micro and macro** level? Could the strategies in this chapter be used to help you to save **Spoons**, and can you combine any of the strategies with our **Common sensory** approach?

Remember that you can also make a note of strategies from other chapters in this space – think outside the box and consider how other strategies from elsewhere in the book might also help you to thrive when public speaking.

Further resources

In order to make the most of the **Safety net** strategies for presenting and public speaking, see Template 21: The safety net approach to presenting and public speaking in **Chapter 10**.

- The following resource from the Harvard Division of Continuing Education provides ten top tips for improving your public speaking: https://professional.dce.harvard.edu/blog/10-tips-for-improving-your-public-speaking-skills

- This resource from the National Social Anxiety Center explores how normal it is to be scared of public speaking and how you might overcome the anxieties associated with it: https://nationalsocialanxietycenter.com/2017/02/20/public-speaking-and-fear-of-brain-freezes

- Medical professionals – as discussed in the Prologue, this book is not a therapeutic book. Its aim is to act as a preventative toolkit, so we strongly encourage you to reach out for professional and medical help should you find yourself in a position where you feel unable to present or speak publicly.

9

The hurdle-free approach to group work

Anticipate, plan for and manage the challenges of working with others

Is this chapter for me?

- Do you dread the thought of working with others but struggle to work out why and what you can do to make group work less stressful?

- Have you ever felt that it is difficult to find efficient ways of working as a team when completing an assigned group work task?

- Do you often feel like you don't get the chance to play to your strengths during group work tasks or fear that you are not in control of ensuring you get a good group grade?

The hurdle-free approach to group work: The big picture

Collaborative work is an important and invaluable feature of learning. Throughout our lives, we will need to be able to work effectively with others – including those that we have chosen to work with, as well as those that we haven't! You may be lucky and find that you enjoy working in a group, but it is not uncommon to find working with others difficult and challenging. Even if you do enjoy group work, it is unlikely to occur without the group encountering some hurdles.

You're likely to have heard of the phrase 'there's no I in team'. However, this is not always helpful and doesn't capture the reality that a group is made up of individuals with different personalities, strengths, needs and ways of thinking and working. When working as a group, it's vital to find ways of working which allow all group members to thrive, rather than just survive the process. The key to effective group work is to be realistic and acknowledge these differences, drawing on this diversity as a strength which can be harnessed.

The **Hurdle-free approach to group work** provides you with strategies which can help your group better anticipate, plan for and manage the hurdles you may face as a team. Approaching group work flexibly, through selecting and combining strategies to develop your own **Combo** that works for your context, will ensure you are able to hit the ground running and take each hurdle in your stride.

In this chapter, we will introduce you to a range of practical strategies to help you to:

- Apply the **3 Cs of effective group work** to remove some of the common group work hurdles from the off!
- Overcome group work hurdles effortlessly by using the **Strategies to help you take group work in your stride**

Don't forget to think about how you can apply all of the different tools you have available to you from the **Welldoing toolkit** when you are considering the strategies in this chapter.

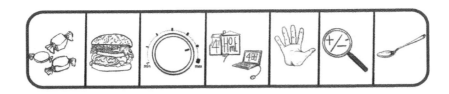

Check in on your Welldoing... Commonly experienced feelings associated with group work

Before we get started, it might be helpful to think about some of the hurdles you might personally experience when working with others in a group. People often see group work as one seemingly insurmountable challenge. In reality, there are often *numerous* smaller hurdles which, when combined together, can leave us feeling like it will be hard for us to stay on track. By reflecting on some of the challenges that may lie ahead based on our own prior experiences, worries or fears, we can start to get a clearer picture of which aspects of group work present the greatest barriers to us. The following 'what if's' are examples of some of the things that learners commonly worry about when faced with the prospect of working in a group. Use this Check in on your Welldoing as an opportunity to reflect on and break down some of the things that might personally be bothering you linked to working in a group. Breaking down the hurdles in this way will then help you to better identify which strategies will be most useful to you (and your group) in the long run.

- What if I let others down and can't complete the work I need to contribute in the timescales we agreed?
- What if I get asked to do something I don't feel I can do?
- What if I disagree with others in the group?
- What if I feel like I am the odd one out or that I have nothing to contribute to the group?
- What if others in the group think I don't know my subject or lack the skills?
- What if others see how shy I am?
- What if I am not heard and my views and opinions are overlooked?
- What if others think the way I work is not 'normal'?
- What if others don't pull their weight and I have to do more work than is fair?
- What if I can't control the process and others undermine my chance of getting a good grade?

Don't run before you can walk! The 3 Cs of effective group work

Whilst people might have similar needs and experience some of the same challenges, group work is complicated by the fact that there are a number of *individuals* involved who may all face slightly different hurdles. Therefore, it can be difficult to unpick and identify the specific issues which are contributing to any challenges the group is facing. Consequently, it becomes quite difficult to recognise which strategies may be most effective at helping the group to overcome these hurdles. By working together as a group to dissect and understand any potential hurdles, you can better anticipate and plan to mitigate against them. Our **3 Cs of effective group work** will help your team to take a running jump when your group work task or project begins.

To do this, consider employing the three Cs of **Consider**, **Communicate** and **Collaborate** (see **Figure 9.1**). These provide you with a structured way of working so that you can successfully bridge the gap between the needs of each individual *and* the needs of the whole group. Using the 3 Cs does not need to become an onerous process which takes a lot of time. Engaging in the process *before* you start completing the work itself will save you all invaluable time and energy in the long run and help to ensure the smooth running of the group!

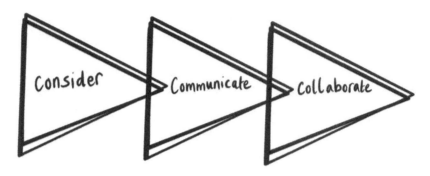

Figure 9.1   The 3 Cs of group work

CAPTION: Consider, communicate and collaborate for group work.

You can also use the 3 Cs as a quick way of checking-in with one another whenever the group feels this could be useful to take stock and see if any new hurdles are on the horizon. This will help you to work flexibly in a group and more readily adapt *throughout* the group work process, based on the changing needs of each group member and the different challenges which may emerge whilst working together.

Consider

This step involves individually considering and thinking about the **Strategies listed below which are designed to help you take group work in your stride**. It's sensible to focus on one or two priority strategies which will be potentially useful for you. For example, you might like to consider the importance of environment or how you might best distribute the work to be carried out. Refer to our **3 Cs of group work** template in **Chapter 10 (Template 20)** to help you to note down your individual thoughts/concerns or ideas linked to a particular aspect of group work which is important to the individuals in the group.

Communicate

After taking time to think about your own individual needs and situation in relation to specific aspects of group working, share these with each other. By communicating with each other about specific aspects of group work, you will start to engage in a realistic and honest approach to determining how you might go about working effectively together. You can use **Template 20** to briefly collate each group member's individual preferences.

Collaborate

Now that you've considered and communicated your individual thoughts, you can start to harness this to work out how you will work together and accommodate the group's diverse needs. For example, can you spot any commonalities or any differences in the way group members like to work? How can you make the most of this knowledge to ensure the group can work together effectively and efficiently?

Bear in mind

Remember, it will not always be possible to create the perfect working conditions for every member of the group. The **3 Cs** strategy can help the group to actively engage with hurdles which may not be explicitly apparent and develop a solution-focused approach to overcoming these.

Strategies for Hurdle-free group work
Manage the environment

When considering how the group is going to function, it is worth paying attention to *how* you plan to work as a group rather than simply focusing entirely on *what* you are going to be working on. For example, you might like to consider timings in terms of when you are going to meet up or where your meetings are likely to be held. This is important in terms of both practical considerations (for example, all being free at the same time and able to travel to the place you are meeting up) and in terms of how factors such as time of day or where you meet may also impact on an individual member's ability to contribute and function effectively in the group context.

In the **Cognitively comfy learning** chapter, we focus on how factors such as the environment, timings for working and type of task can impact on our focus, concentration and motivation. Although working in a group makes it more difficult to create the perfect working conditions for every member of the group all of the time, being more aware of how such factors affect us and bearing this in mind when planning can help us to better anticipate and mitigate for those factors which might otherwise be easily overlooked. For example, if one member of the group is adversely affected by background noise, repeatedly meeting in a busy and potentially overwhelming environment such as a coffee shop could inadvertently undermine the group dynamic and affect some individuals' perceived behaviour and contribution.

If you feel that you are likely to be adversely affected by factors such as the environment, don't be afraid to let others know and see if it is possible to adapt or adjust the environment. See **Cognitively comfy learning** in **Chapter 3** for strategies to help with this. In most cases, other group members would rather you were in a position to work comfortably than not be able to work. For example, if you share a working space, others may not mind if the door is open or closed but for you it might make a big difference. Being open with one another and encouraging a better understanding of the things we find challenging are explored further in the **Share your Achilles' heel** strategy on the following page.

Strategies to help you take group work in your stride

Sign on the dotted line...

Drawing up a contract for all team members to sign can be a very useful strategy to ensure that everyone is on the same page and clear expectations and parameters are established from the start. When putting together a contract, it is important that all group members contribute to and agree on what is set so that everyone feels invested.

It is important to make sure the contract is realistic and builds in a degree of flexibility as it can be tempting to draw up a contract which is based on an idealised way of working. For example, you might like to build in flexible deadlines or flexible percentages for how much work people need to output so that deadlines become achievable and sustainable.

You might also like to draw on the **Share your Achilles' heel** strategy so that each group member feels comfortable and able to communicate the barriers that might cause a challenge for them. Factoring in a **Plan B** (see the following page) could also enable you to safeguard against things not going to plan. The aim is for your group contract to directly reflect the needs of the group, as well as the overall aims or goals of the project. It enables the contract to work with the group members, rather than against them if a problem arises, and helps you to plan for and mitigate against any hurdles before they undermine the effectiveness of the group project.

Plan B

As mentioned previously, it can be quite common in a group working context to want to launch straight in and hit the ground running, particularly if time is short or the work being assessed is high stakes. However, spending a little more time anticipating and planning for potential problems, although it may seem counter-intuitive, can really help to save time and energy in the long run. Plan B encourages the group to put in place a backup plan for when things don't run smoothly or go to plan! For example, this might include identifying a primary person to work on a particular task, but then also identifying a backup buddy to help out if a problem occurs or the primary person feels they have hit a hurdle. This reduces the potential for the team to struggle with tasks on their own and builds in flexibility to the plan from the very start, recognising that learning isn't always straightforward and hurdles or barriers are commonplace.

Share your Achilles' heel

This strategy can be used to help prompt honest conversations about aspects of group work or learning you all find more challenging. As mentioned previously, we may feel pressure to present the best version of ourselves when working in a group context; we may worry that others might identify a weakness in us or think less of us if we do not represent the perfect team player. In reality, the whole point of group working is to share responsibility for a project and to combine skills so that the team functions as a whole. This means that we can in fact draw on different skills from each individual so that there is no longer pressure on each person to be 'perfect' or offer the whole package of skills. Therefore, try and remind each other that the whole point of the team approach is to combine skills, divide and conquer the different tasks and match roles and tasks to different people's strengths. We often think about our strengths and weaknesses in isolation but it is useful to recognise that these are often linked. It can be really helpful and a great relief to let others know what we find challenging.

Great minds don't think alike: Thinking outside the box

There is increasing recognition that 'great minds' do not think alike (Syed, 2022). Group working often involves a complex range of skills in order to break down tasks, problem-solve and find solutions and effectively convey these ideas to others. Having diversity in terms of thinking can really help us to challenge or reframe our own stance. Therefore, an important aspect of group work is working with people who are potentially very different from us, whether that is linked to subject knowledge, culture, background or the way in which we learn and work. Working in this way provides us with vital experience of working with others which prepares us for life and work beyond learning. But there is an important distinction between working with others and working with others *well*. Simply being open to and tolerant of difference, whilst really important, does not guarantee that group work will be successful for a diverse group; if we better understand the different ways in which we think, live and work, we can anticipate and harness this difference as a strength.

Group agreement is necessary to an extent to help ensure the group's success, but an essential ingredient of group working is that we also need to stretch each other and help each other to develop. Different viewpoints or perceptions can be a very powerful mechanism to ensure the group work evolves.

Big picture or fine details?

Like **Great minds don't think alike** (previous section), a common hurdle of effective group working is that some of us are naturally big picture thinkers and like to consider seeing a project as a whole before committing to the detail. In contrast, some of us prefer to dive in and consider the fine details of the work. Neither approach is right or wrong and both types of thinking are required for a group task to be effective. Recognising this difference in thinking and then, importantly, harnessing it in the way the group works can help the group to effectively move between the 'big picture' and the 'details'. The task can then be managed in a way that is comfortable for everyone in the group.

Revisiting Breaking it down, Done lists and the Progress checker

Make sure the tasks that you put on your to-do list are achievable and enable you to see progress. When faced with the hurdle of a task that has an unclear outcome or for which progress is difficult to measure, people often stall. Revisit the **Breaking it down, To do Done lists** and **Progress checker** strategies in **Chapter 3**. In summary, it can be very helpful to break down tasks to a certain level of detail to allow them to be wholly understood and achievable. For example, rather than writing 'do report' or 'gather information', try breaking these tasks down into manageable bitesize chunks.

If you are worried you are not making progress or are not going to complete a task on time, then try and use percentages to help show your progress. This is much better than avoiding a meeting for fear of having to say you have not completed something on time. Note that you can also use these strategies as a way of helping to set a realistic goal in terms of what you can achieve before your next meeting (e.g. I can realistically achieve another 10%). Remember that if you don't like percentages, you could use colour coding instead.

Student voices

' Using the **Breaking it down** and **Done lists** strategies really helped with group work because this enabled us to make sure we had equally divided the tasks, made sure we were clear on what was expected of us as individuals and helped us to see progress.

Rosa, A Levels, UK '

Equal contribution

One of the greatest challenges associated with group work is the idea that everyone should make an equal contribution to the project to ensure its success and avoid most of the work falling to specific individuals. The difficulty with striving for equal contribution is that this can be very hard to define and measure, and as such this can lead to tension within the group. For example, it could be that time spent on the project could provide an indicator of how much work each person has contributed, but people work at different speeds and therefore one individual may produce the same output as someone else in half the time. Some members of the group might be great at generating content, but others' roles and contributions may be less obvious as they have generated ideas or spent time 'thinking' etc.

It is therefore worth considering equal contribution in broader terms which takes into account the various and often nuanced ways in which we can contribute to the process of group work. Try to view contribution as something which fluctuates rather than something which is static, perhaps like a relay race where the group can harness each individual's focus, energy and motivation at a different time or stage in the working process.

Product versus process model of group working

When allocating tasks to group members, we can inadvertently ask every group member to carry out every task involved in meeting the project deliverables. Consider the metaphor of friends cooking a meal together – if the meal is divided up so that every person has to make a dish then *every* person has to write a shopping list, go to the shops, mix the ingredients, do the cooking… This isn't always the most efficient and effective way to achieve the overall end goal. Before dividing tasks for group work, think about whether to divide tasks by *processes* and match these to each person's individual skill set. For example, those who are good at researching information could lead on this, whereas those who are good at writing could put their energy into drafting the report. In other words, you will be working in a way which plays to your strengths and supporting each other more.

Dabble strategy and tricky tasks

The **Dabble** strategy and **Tricky tasks** strategy presented in **Chapter 3** can help to overcome the hurdle of 'getting started' with a task. Rather than thinking 'I must do some work', use the Dabble strategy and try working on one bit for a few moments – if this doesn't work, step away and then try 'Dabbling' with another task instead. It can also be helpful to identify tasks which you may have trouble completing, or ones where you might need help or input from someone else – we call these **Tricky tasks**.

The authors' approach to Welldoing

We all have different preferred ways of working and this changes depending on our circumstances. We have had to rely heavily on this chapter to help us work effectively as a team to write this book. We often use the **3 Cs** so we can consider each other's needs, communicate this to one another and find ways to collaborate. We have found it really helpful to recognise that we all have different strengths and we have actively sought to draw on this so we can achieve our goals as a group, rather than each person having to be the perfect all-rounder.

Key take aways

- Remember that when working as a group everyone has individual needs, preferences and strengths. Keeping this in mind and finding ways to work that take this into account can often help to overcome common group work hurdles.

- Always remember the **3 Cs** of effective group work – **consider, communicate and collaborate**.

- Make sure you're all on the same page, using strategies such as **Sign on the dotted line**, and think about the why and how of the task you need to collectively achieve, not just the 'what'. This will mean you need to think about the environment you will be working in and revisit strategies such as **Breaking it down**, **Done lists** and **Progress checker** as well as the **Product versus process model of group working**.

My blank canvas

Use this space to make a note of strategies you think could be  useful to help you make group working hurdle-free. Remember to **Pick and mix**, **Develop your combo** and **Turn up (or down) the dial**, so that you can personalise an approach that works for you.

Don't forget that you may find some of your favourite strategies from this chapter help you to apply **Welldoing4home** and **Welldoing4work**. Similarly, can any of the strategies you have selected be applied at a **Micro and macro** level? Could the strategies in this chapter be used to help you to save **Spoons**, and can you combine any of the strategies with our **Common sensory** approach?

Remember that you can also make a note of strategies from other chapters in this space – think outside the box and consider how other strategies from elsewhere in the book might also help you to overcome any group working hurdles!

Further resources

- In order to make the most of the strategies in this chapter, see the following templates in **Chapter 10**:

  o   Template 20: The 3 Cs of effective group work

- This resource gives some general tips on effective group working: www.birming ham.ac.uk/schools/metallurgy-materials/about/cases/group-work/tips.aspx

10

Tempting templates
Example templates
to help you put Welldoing
into practice

Tempting templates: The big picture

Our **Tempting templates** chapter provides you with example templates as well as space to help you put your own approaches to Welldoing into practice. The templates we have included here have been used and developed in conjunction with students. Please feel free to use the templates in the suggested format or to make adaptions so that they reflect your needs.  Use the templates and space provided as a starting point, a blank canvas to get creative, rather than being limited by what we have demonstrated on the page.

We mention throughout the book that our needs fluctuate and change over time depending on the context we are studying in and how we feel. Therefore, you may find the type and style of template you require changes and evolves to reflect your changing needs. Also remember that a template you find helpful to support your thinking for an aspect of your study may be easily adapted and applied in other areas of your life. Remember that any Welldoing for learning strategies which are working for you, may also be transferable and support you with your **Welldoing4home** and **Welldoing4work**.

Template 1: The common sensory approach to Welldoing

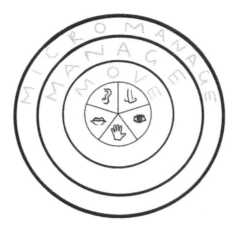

Use the sensory wheel to help you to think about how you might use your environment to your advantage to boost your motivation and concentration. Think about what *your* ideal working environment might look like, whether this is in the form of a particular spot in your home, a busy coffee shop or somewhere outside (**Move**). Also reflect on how you might be able to harness your senses and adapt your environment to make learning as comfortable as possible (see the **Manage** and **Micro-manage** approaches to harnessing your environment).

Remember, you can use the **Common sensory approach to Welldoing** for any context in your life and harness your senses to support your study, employment and home life.

Don't forget all of the different tools you have available to you from the **Welldoing toolkit**.

Template 2: Manage your time rather than your time managing you

If you feel that the *time has come* for you to start managing your time more effectively, then use this template to help you. We have provided a template which includes seven days a week. Remember to tailor the timetable itself so that it works for you. Feel free to change the times or days of the week it covers and the length of the blocks of time themselves; the whole point of this aspect of Welldoing is to plan your time in a way that is flexible, adaptable and responsive to your changing needs.

Remember to **Pick and mix** the approaches we suggest; **Block**, **Buffer** and **Chunk** your time as required and don't forget to add in some **Bored**, **Break** and **Stolen time** if helpful. The template can be used to get you started but your timetable should not be fixed, rather it can evolve and shift as your needs change. See this as a fluid space which you can revisit *time and time* again to tweak your timetable!

Don't forget all of the different tools you have available to you from the **Welldoing toolkit**.

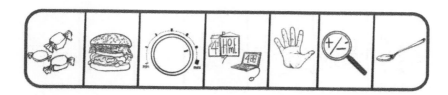

Template 3: Break it down! How to make tasks more manageable

Use this template to practise breaking down tasks to make them easier to tackle. Keep breaking the task down until it is at a level you can cope with. For example, if you have a report to tackle, keep breaking this down into smaller steps such as *write introduction section* or *capture points I want to make for introduction* or even *set up template to capture ideas for introduction!* It doesn't matter if the steps seem too small, this will help you to overcome that overwhelming sense of how to get started and let you connect with the task at hand.

And remember that just as you can use the **Break it down** strategy to tackle a piece of work you have to complete for your studies, you can use the same approach to tackle *any* task you are finding it hard to face, whether this is at work or linked to something you need to carry out at home.

Don't forget all of the different tools you have available to you from the **Welldoing toolkit.**

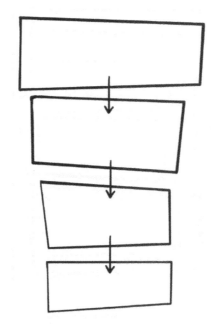

Template 4: Break it down! How to organise tasks by type

Once we have got into the habit of breaking tasks down into manageable chunks, we can also take control of tasks by starting to group them based on what we might need to do to complete them and how many Spoons we might use in the process. Use the designated spaces below to identify your **Breadth and Depth tasks**, your **Quick wins**, your **Tricky tasks** and tasks that lend themselves to **Batching**.

Don't forget all of the different tools you have available to you from the **Welldoing toolkit**.

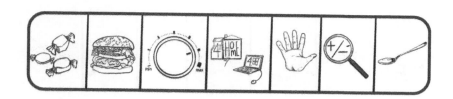

Template 5: Taking note of your progress

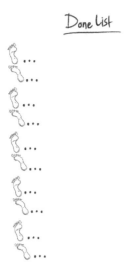

When life feels like a never-ending to-do list, it can be really helpful to produce a **Done list** instead! This can help you to gain a sense of achievement and also boost your motivation as you take note of the progress you have made. Use the space above to help yourself to take note of the steps you have completed, no matter how seemingly small – small steps will quickly begin to accumulate and move you in the right direction. List the things you have done rather than those you haven't and take some satisfaction from crossing out tasks to reinforce the progress you are making.

Don't forget that you can also make a note of progress for multiple aspects of life, beyond a list of tasks – you might like to record progress in terms of the time spent doing something or to acknowledge that you have made progress working towards a goal you have set yourself related to an aspect of your life you would like to actively change.

You may also like to use the space above to draw an image (which you can add to over time) which helps you to visually record your progress, whether in the form of footsteps or a growing tree; be creative and find a way of registering the distance you have travelled.

Don't forget all of the different tools you have available to you from the **Welldoing toolkit**.

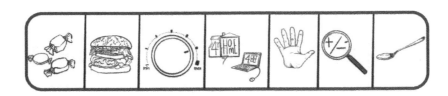

Template 6: Save our spoons!

Use this page to make a note of strategies from throughout the book (as well as your own) which help you to save your Spoons! Remember, this might include strategies that make you more comfortable to learn, strategies that help you to prioritise and save much-needed energy or ones that help you to work smart rather than hard. You might also like to make a note of long-term Spoon-saving strategies which help you to study and live in a way that is sustainable, as well as those strategies you might need to draw on for short periods of time when life is piling on the pressure and you need to give yourself a break.

Don't forget all of the different tools you have available to you from the **Welldoing toolkit**.

....

....

....

....

....

....

....

....

....

Template 7: Prioritising pressures

When the pressures mount and you need to take action, use this template to use the 4Ds and help you prioritise tasks and decide which tasks you can **Do, defer, delegate and delete**. Remember that you can also save spoons by doing some things less well!

Don't forget all of the different tools you have available to you from the **Welldoing toolkit.**

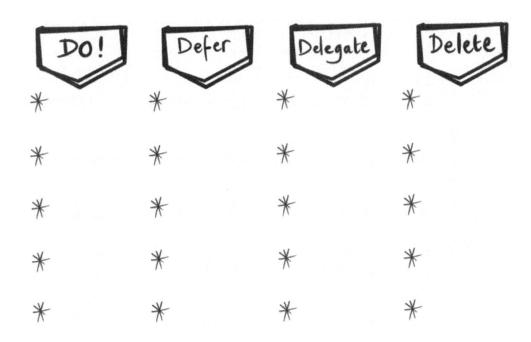

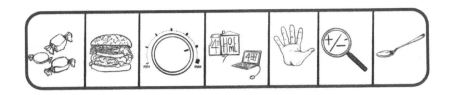

Template 8: Worry work-out

If your worries are getting in the way, undermining your confidence or stopping you from moving forwards, then try our worry work-out to help you problem-solve your worries. Can you find a way to break down your worries into smaller, more focused and manageable challenges to solve? Can you prioritise which worry to tackle first and which to park for later? Can you harness your senses to help you stop over thinking? Use the space below to unpick your worries.

Don't forget all of the different tools you have available to you from the **Welldoing toolkit**.

....

....

....

....

....

....

....

....

....

....

Template 9: Sleep survival

In an ideal world, we should establish good sleep hygiene strategies to ensure we get a good night's sleep. But sometimes our sleep goes awry, which can itself become an added pressure. Use this space to make a note of the strategies that you can draw upon when your sleep is not at its best.

Don't forget all of the different tools you have available to you from the **Welldoing toolkit**.

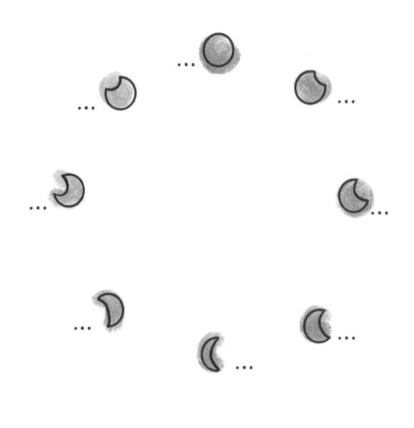

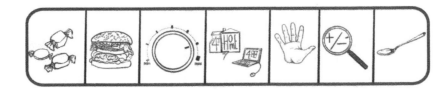

Template 10: Active relaxing

The more stressed we get, the harder it can be to take a step back, switch off and unwind. Use our active relaxing template to help you consider where, when and how you might be able to give your ability to relax a boost.

Don't forget all of the different tools you have available to you from the **Welldoing toolkit.**

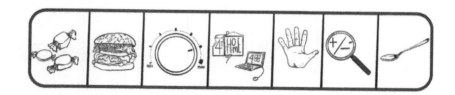

Template 11: Fear of the blank page

Use this blank space to explore how you can tailor and adapt the blank page in front of you to support your thinking and writing. Can you divide and conquer the space to make it seem less overwhelming; can you make it mucky to make it feel less perfect? Could you use colour or images to help overcome fear of the blank page?

Don't forget all of the different tools you have available to you from the **Welldoing toolkit**.

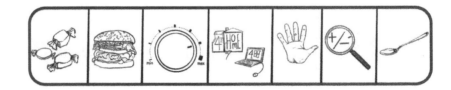

Template 12: Thinking spaces – The mind map

Use this space to make a mind map, whether you are getting started on a piece of work and need to generate some ideas or if you need to better understand a complex topic and want to see how different ideas relate to each other. Remember you can also use images and colour to help you organise your ideas or thoughts, as mind maps don't have to be captured in words alone.

If the mind map works for you for study-related tasks, remember that it may also be useful when planning or capturing your thoughts more generally for other areas of your life, such as if you have to plan the contents of a letter or break down and 'see' a challenge you are facing.

Don't forget all of the different tools you have available to you from the **Welldoing toolkit**.

Template 13: Thinking spaces – Thinking inside the box

Use this table method when you need to ensure you have absolute control over your planning or if you are feeling overwhelmed by a piece of work and need to break it down into more manageable sections. The table below represents only one way of using this method, combined with using a formula to help structure and sequence planning and writing. Feel free to adapt the number of rows, columns and headings. Think inside the box and get creative to boost your thinking and planning!

Remember that if this method works for you for planning assignments, it may also help you manage other areas of your life such as making shopping or planning lists for home.

Don't forget all of the different tools you have available to you from the **Welldoing toolkit**.

Paragraph	Point	Information	Explain	So what?
1.				
2.				
3.				
4.				
5.				

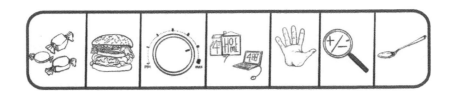

Template 14: Note-taking

Use this space to get creative with your approach to note-taking. Remember, as you are trying a new approach for the first time, you might like to practise it first whilst studying so you can set your own pace, rather than attempting to change the way you take notes in a fast-paced lecture where you may feel the stakes are too high! Feel free to adapt the space below so that the page shapes and supports your thinking. Consider using pictorial notes, colour, shorthand and space on the page to boost your organisation of the information.

Don't forget all of the different tools you have available to you from the **Welldoing toolkit**.

Template 15: Cracking the recipe of assignment briefs and examination questions

Use this space to actively draw out the key things you need to cover in your assignment using the assignment brief and/or marking criteria. List the key ingredients you need to include, e.g. whether you need to compare, contrast, analyse or evaluate.

Work out how you can include these ingredients *throughout* your paragraphs rather than separating this out into separate sections of the assignment. For example, if the assignment asks you to *analyse*, it is better to weave the analysis throughout the assignment in each paragraph, rather than putting this all at the end. Don't forget to refer to our **PIES: Recipe for a tasty paragraph** in **Chapter 6** to help you with this. Get creative and use the space to map out how you might start to answer the question. Remember to use the space to scribble key words, to draw, to doodle, to link and to explore how you might answer the question before you actually come up with a plan or start writing it.

Don't forget all of the different tools you have available to you from the **Welldoing toolkit**.

Title.

Key ingredients.

-
-
-
-
-

I need to include topic of subject, methods I need to use such as 'analyse', 'evaluate', 'reflect', etc. Note any resources I need to refer to such as key data, a policy, theory, report or approach I need to apply (use title and brief to help identify this).

Pies mix.

Think about how the ingredients listed above might need to be included in your paragraphs. For example, if you are evaluating or analysing, how can you make sure that you do so consistently in every paragraph? If you are referring to key themes or key sources of information, is it better to separate this out into different sections or paragraphs or sprinkle this throughout your paragraphs? You might like to adapt your PIES mix formula to make sure it helps you to stay on track and include the key ingredients needed to answer the assignment question and meet the aims of the brief.

Taste test.

← Remember to taste test your writing! Check that your paragraphs contain the 'right' ingredients in the right amount and that you have answered the question. Note any reminders here to help you go back and taste test your work.

Template 16: Reading shopping baskets

Use the template on the facing page to help you stay in control of the information you are looking for when reading, finding useful sources and identifying materials to evidence your thinking. Remember to do a quick calculation using our **Basic recipe for sources** in **Chapter 6**. This will help to ensure you don't spend too long gathering hundreds of possible materials when reading.

Use the Reading shopping basket template to store the most important, relevant or useful materials you have read, rather than over-filling your brain (and potentially your assignment) with shopping trolleys full of nice materials which don't actually add to or develop your work. The sources column will help you to stay in control of making a note of the sources of information you are using so that you can make sure your referencing also goes to plan!

Don't forget all of the different tools you have available to you from the **Welldoing toolkit**.

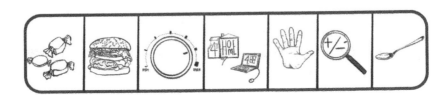

Tasty quote/idea/image/ diagram that may be of use	Source taken from (add reference details/link here)

Template 17: Reading shopping lists

Make a reading 'shopping list' below (based on the assignment brief/topic/marking criteria) to make sure you stay on track and keep your reading focused; you may come across lots of interesting ideas, but try to keep to the list and focus on key ideas that directly correlate to the piece of work you are focused on. If you do come across additional interesting ideas that you think it would be useful to capture somewhere and store for later, then remember to also look at the **Ideas freezer** template (**Template 18**), the ideal space to store on ice all those extra ideas, quotes or sources of information for when you need them later.

Don't forget all of the different tools you have available to you from the **Welldoing toolkit**.

*

*

*

*

*

*

*

*

*

Template 18: The ideas freezer

Use this space to capture or 'freeze' the additional ideas that pop into your head when you are in the middle of writing or planning. It is important to keep hold of those ideas, but by storing them in your ideas freezer, you reduce the risk of a new idea sending your writing off on a tangent! Get creative and fill your freezer, safe in the knowledge that your ideas are stored safely 'on ice' for when you might need them.

Don't forget all of the different tools you have available to you from the **Welldoing toolkit**.

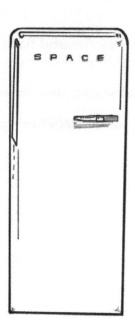

Template 19: The revision elevator – putting in the groundwork

Use the template on the facing page to help you break down your revision into manageable chunks. Remember that using a syllabus overview might help with this and save you time in terms of identifying all the topics.

Tailor the columns to support the type of progress you want to measure. You could use a column for understand, memorise and apply to make sure you cover all the key aspects that make up effective revision, rather than just using the topic list as a guide to what you have memorised. You can also use colours or emojis to make a note of your progress. Don't worry if it doesn't feel like you are always making steady progress – progress is not always linear and neat and tidy. It is more likely to occur in sudden bursts. If you are feeling that progress overall is definitely slower than you would like then broaden the range of strategies you are using to boost your efficiency.

Remember to also use the **Memory elevator** as well as the other **Ground floor** and **Top floor** strategies to help you to tick or mark off how much you understand, have memorised and applied.

This template may work particularly well with **Template 2: Manage your time rather than your time managing you**.

Don't forget all of the different tools you have available to you from the **Welldoing toolkit**.

Topic/Subtopic	Understand.	Memorised	Applied.
	☺	☺	

Template 20: The 3 Cs of group work

Use the below template to help you to better consider, understand and plan for different needs within the group. Remember that you won't always be able to meet everyone's needs all the time, but you can work towards identifying the little things that you may be able to manage and control which might impact positively or negatively on the group's experience as a whole.

Use the space to **Consider** each individual's needs, to **Communicate** these in a way that might helpfully inform the group's planning and better **Collaborate** by harnessing each other's individual strengths and preferred ways of working in order to ensure the group works as efficiently and effectively as possible.

Don't forget all of the different tools you have available to you from the **Welldoing toolkit**.

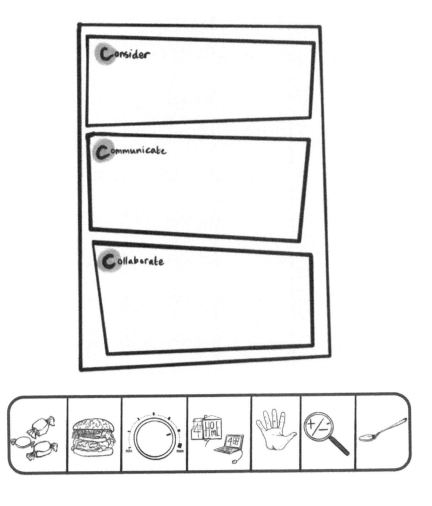

Template 21: The safety net approach to presenting and public speaking

Use the safety nets to work out your **Combo** for making presenting or public speaking more manageable. Remember that having a number of strategies at your disposal which you can use simultaneously is likely to be more beneficial than having just one or two. Also remember to **Turn up (or down) the dial** on the safety nets you chose to increase their impact.

Don't forget all of the different tools you have available to you from the **Welldoing toolkit**.

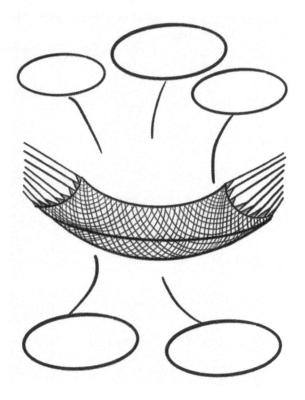

Template 22: Welldoing your way!

Use this blank space to pull together all your favourite Welldoing strategies into one place! Refer back to any notes you have made in the **My blank canvas** space in each chapter. Skim and scan the book, dipping in and out to find your go-to strategies.

Remember that Welldoing works best when we combine strategies from across the book: a strategy for boosting memory in the **Revision elevator** chapter may work best when combined with a couple of strategies from **Cognitively comfy learning** or **Time and task savvy learning**.

Don't forget all of the different tools you have available to you from the **Welldoing toolkit**.

....

....

....

....

....

....

....

....

....

....

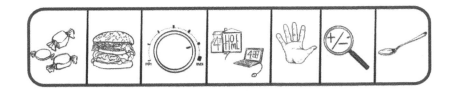

Template 23: Take your Welldoing up a level

Sometimes we need to rely on different strategies than our usual go-to approaches, particularly if we are feeling under pressure or finding everything a bit challenging. Ironically, we often forget the most important strategies when we need them the most! Use the template below to help you think about the different strategies you may need to rely on as your circumstances or how you feel change.

Use the first level of the triangle to make a note of useful day-to-day strategies you can build into your routine. Use the next level for strategies when the pressure is mounting and you need to pull on some extra support to get you through. Use the top level of the triangle to make a note of those strategies you can use when most in need – this might be when you are feeling stressed, overwhelmed or burnt out. These might be your emergency strategies that you need for very short periods of time, such as before presenting or a deadline or for longer periods if you need to give yourself a bit of space and take the pressure off.

Don't forget all of the different tools you have available to you from the **Welldoing toolkit**.

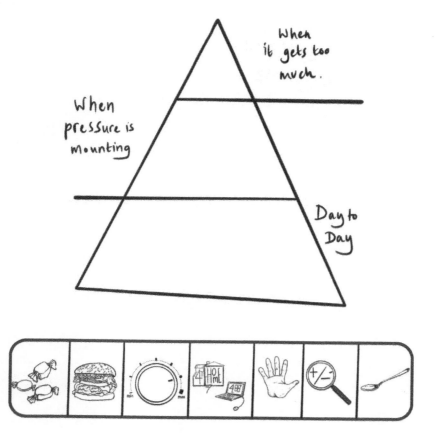

References

Prologue

World Health Organization (WHO). (2022). *How to find and use health information.* www.who.int/tools/your-life-your-health/how-to-find-and-use-health-information

Chapter 1: Welcome to Welldoing

Hora, M.T. & Oleson, A.K. (2017). Examining study habits in undergraduate STEM courses from a situative perspective. *International Journal of STEM Education, 4,* 1. https://doi.org/10.1186/s40594-017-0055-6

Miserandino, C. (2020). *The Spoon Theory.* https://lymphoma-action.org.uk/sites/default/files/media/documents/2020-05/Spoon%20theory%20by%20Christine%20Miserandino.pdf

Sauvé, L., Fortin, A., Viger, C. & Landry, F. (2016). Ineffective learning strategies: A significant barrier to post-secondary perseverance. *Journal of Further and Higher Education, 42*(2), 205–222.

Chapter 2: Cognitively comfy learning

Gallwey, W.T. (1974). *The inner game books.* https://theinnergame.com/inner-game-books

Oppezzo, M. & Schwartz, D.L. (2014). Give your ideas some legs: The positive effect of walking on creative thinking. *Journal of Experimental Psychology: Learning, Memory, and Cognition, 40*(4), 1142–1152.

Chapter 3: Time and task savvy learning

Aeon, B., Faber, A. & Panaccio, A. (2021) *Does time management work? A meta-analysis.* PLoS One. Jan 11;*16*(1).

Dierdorff, E.C. (2020) *Time management is about more than life hacks.* Harvard Business Review. https://hbr.org/2020/01/time-management-is-about-more-than-life-hacks

Chapter 4: Stress-free learning (well almost!)

Canfield, J., Hansen, M.V. & Hewitt, L. (2013). *The power of focus: How to hit your business, personal and financial targets with confidence and certainty.* Vermillion.

Farrand, P., Woodfood, J. & Small, F. (2019). *Managing your worries.* University of Exeter.

Chapter 5: Reader's and writer's block

Mehelin, N. (2022). *Three tips to tackle reader's block.* https://blogs.lse.ac.uk/studentsatlse/2022/05/01/three-tips-to-tackle-readers-block

Morehead, K., Dunlosky, J., Rawson, K., Blasiman R. & Hollis, R. (2019). Note-taking habits of 21st century college students: Implications for student learning, memory, and achievement. *Memory, 27*(6), 807–819.

Chapter 6: Recipes for planning and writing

Kolb, D.A. (1984). *Experiential learning: Experience as the source of learning and development.* Prentice-Hall.

Schon, D.A. (1991). *The reflective practitioner.* Ashgate Publishing.

Sweller, J. (1988). Cognitive load during problem solving: Effects on learning. *Cognitive Science, 12*, 257–285.

University of Portsmouth (2022). *Better essays: Signposting.* www.port.ac.uk/student-life/help-and-advice/study-skills/written-assignments/better-essays-signposting

Chapter 7: The revision elevator

Bruner, J. (1996). *The culture of education*. Harvard University Press.
Caviglioli, O. (2022). *Visual clarity*. www.olicav.com
Clark, J.M. & Paivio, A. (1991). Dual coding theory and education. *Educational Psychology Review, 3*(3), 149–170.
Madan, C.R. & Singhal, A. (2012). Using actions to enhance memory: Effects of enactment, gestures, and exercise on human memory. *Frontiers in Psychology, 19*(3), 507.
Rodeiro, C.V. & Macinska, S. (2022). *Teachers' and students' views of access arrangements in high-stakes assessments*. BERA conference, Liverpool, 5–8 September. www.cambridgeassessment.org.uk/Images/663225-teachers-and-students-views-of-access-arrangements-in-high-stakes-assessments.pdf
Weinstein, Y., Sumeracki, M. & Caviglioli, O. (2018). *Understanding how we learn: A visual guide* (1st edn). Routledge.

Chapter 8: Walking a tightrope

British Council. (2022). *How to overcome your fear of public speaking*. www.british council.org/voices-magazine/how-overcome-fear-public-speaking

Chapter 9: The hurdle-free approach to group work

Syed, M. (2022). *Supercharge your leadership with cognitive diversity*. www.matthewsyed.co.uk/supercharge-your-leadership-team-with-cognitive-diversity

Glossary

Active relaxing: Active relaxing can refer specifically to the act of using movement or exercise to aid relaxation. In the Welldoing context, we refer to this as the act of *consciously focusing* on the ways in which we are trying to relax. If we are struggling to switch off and unwind, actively focusing on or being aware of relaxing can help us to connect fully so that we can totally immerse ourselves in this experience. We can also increase our ability to switch off by engaging the brain in a focused activity such as reading, listening to music or exercising.

Analysis paralysis: The inability to make a decision, move forwards or complete a task due to becoming overwhelmed with too much information. We might experience analysis paralysis in relation to our environment or a specific task that we are finding overwhelming or linked to our own thoughts if we are paralysing ourselves through over-thinking.

Cognitive comfort: Understanding that our environment doesn't simply affect our physical comfort linked to learning – e.g. our posture, ability to hear or see. Our environment also shapes our ability to think, process new ideas, retain information and synthesise new ideas. For learning to be effective, we need to make sure we consider both our physical *and* cognitive comfort.

Comfy learning: Ensuring that we harness our environment in order to boost our motivation, focus and concentration, making it easier for us to work smartly in a way that is tailored to our needs.

Common sensory approach: Applying a common sense approach to help us to reflect on how we can actively use our senses (sight, hearing, smell, taste and touch) to better harness our environment to boost motivation, concentration and focus.

Information overload: When our brains are provided with too much information or data and are therefore we are unable to effectively make sense of it, understand it or process it.

Smart study: Adapting the *way* in which you approach learning to ensure that learning becomes as efficient and productive as possible.

Thinking spaces: Just as our environment can influence how we learn, the blank page (physical and digital) can also be harnessed so that it boosts our ability to think and learn. We can shape, structure and manipulate this blank space so that it aids our thinking and boosts our **cognitive comfort**.

Wellbeing: The state of being comfortable, healthy and happy.

Welldoing: Welldoing is essentially about tailoring, adapting and refining the way in which we approach or 'do' tasks in order to help us achieve, thrive and maintain our wellbeing.

Zoom reading: Actively applying strategies to aid our ability to skim and scan when reading to boost our reading efficiency. Zoom reading involves zooming in and out of a text so that we can focus on the words at different levels, whether this is when deciding if a book or chapter is relevant for us, or whether we are zooming in on an individual sentence or word to apply our reading comprehension skills.

Index